Wonder Aces of

ABOUT THE BOOK

Tearing through the skies in death defying feats of air-borne heroism, these ace pilots of World War I pushed back the barriers of human endurance. The dare-devil demands they increasingly made on air technology spearheaded the development of the aircraft industry as we know it.

Major Smithers has selected ten of the world's greatest trail-blazing pilots and described their incredible lives. In a sequence of ripping yarns, he progressively reveals the weird and wonderful combinations of exceptional personality factors which fashioned the wonder aces of the air.

James McCudden, the greatest of all fighter pilots, Jimmy Doolittle the stuntsman who perfected the use of the aircraft carrier, the immortal Edward Rickenbacker Charles Sansom, who founded naval/air warfare, Robert Loraine, W. A. Bishop, Auberon Lucas, Raoul Lufbery, Frank Luke – each has his own gripping story, his own remarkable motives, his own inventive and narrow escapes. Smithers brings them all to life with his familiar gusto for adventure and excitement.

ABOUT THE AUTHOR

Major A. J. Smithers was born in 1919 and served in France, West Africa and the Far East in the Second World War and subsequently as Deputy Assistant General War Crimes in Germany. He has published biographies of Sir Hoder Smith-Dorrien, Sir John Monash, Lord Kitchener, a history of the Kaffir Wars and recently a true-life ripping yarn about Toby Rawlinson.

Wonder Aces of the Air

The Flying Heroes of the Great War

A. J. Smithers

GORDON & CREMONESI

Designed by Heather Gordon

Set in 12 on 14 pt Baskerville
and printed in Great Britain by
The Garden City Press Limited
Letchworth, Hertfordshire SG6 1JS

British Library Cataloguing in Publication Data
Smithers, Alan Jack
  Wonder aces of the air.
  1. European War, 1914–1918 – Aerial operations –
Biography 2. World War, 1939–1945 – Aerial
operations – Biography 3. Air pilots – Biography
1. Title
940.4'4'0922   D600   78–41260
LCCN: 78–041260
ISBN: 0–86033–077–X

Gordon & Cremonesi Publishers
London and New York
New River House
34 Seymour Road
London N8 0BE

Sleep not, my country: though night is here, afar
Your children of the morning are clamorous for war:
Fire in the night, O dreams!
  Though she sends you as she sent you, long ago,
  South to desert, east to ocean, west to snow,
West of these out to seas colder than the Hebrides I must go
  Where the fleet of stars is anchored and the young
  Star-captains glow.

James Elroy Flecker
The Dying Patriot

Acknowledgments

My thanks are due to many people for their help in the writing of this book and these I gratefully tender. To the Librarians of the Royal United Services Institution and of that which in my obsolete way I insist on calling the Air Ministry; to those of the High Commissions for Canada and Australia and of the Embassy of the United States of America. I am indebted to the representatives of the late Lords Douglas of Kirtleside and Tweedsmuir for permission to quote from their printed works and especially so to Lord Tweedsmuir's great-nephew Toby Buchan for reading the script and, more than once, saving me from falling into error.

For the illustrations not my own, my thanks to the Imperial War Museum and my publishers Gordon & Cremonesi.

As to the mistakes, omissions and misjudgments, of which no book has ever been entirely innocent, I claim these for my own.

Acknowledgements

Contents

Introduction

At the end of the nineteenth century the discoveries that had greatly speeded up the long march of mankind were four: the domesticated horse, the wheel, the fore-and-aft sail, and the energy latent in boiling water. Other inventions had been adapted beyond their original purposes. The paddle-wheel that had driven water-mills became, without changing its name, the motive power of early steam ships. Mill sails, by way of the tin windmill that irrigated much of America, became the screw which propelled vessels through the water at great speeds. In the last two decades of a century that began with communications no better than those of Imperial Rome a new factor appeared with the realization that the rock-oil variously called petroleum, gasoline, essence and benzin could be made into a vapour, exploded in a confined space by electricity and thus turn wheels with a power and lightness thitherto unknown. The internal combustion engine, not content with making a new world of road vehicles, provided the means of putting man into the last unused element. Aircraft, built by Hiram Maxim and others, were ready and waiting for it. Now came the means of getting them off the ground and keeping them there.

The process was not painless, for even as the Inquisition had damned Galileo so did less committed men cry down the early fliers. As late as 1910, when Lieutenant Gibbs attempted to give a flying display near Bilbao, a crowd of about 30,000 wrecked his machine and one zealot tried to knife the pilot, asserting loudly that flying was impossible; the crowd encouraged him with chants of: "Down with science; long live religion". Elsewhere the same result was achieved by the simpler expedient of withholding cash. The men who had money lacked faith: the men who had faith lacked money. Even the philosophical Wright brothers were prophets with honour but little else in their own country, especially after Lieutenant Selfridge achieved the melancholy distinction of becoming the first aeroplane casualty when he and Orville Wright crashed in September 1908.

It was in France that internal combustion was best supported. The discovery meant that the motor-car and the flying-machine appeared within a few years of each other and two almost contemporaneous inventions of such magnitude were not easily digestible. The car was within the reach of all men who were moderately well-off and it caught on quickly, though people with cash enough to spare for this luxury were usually past their youth and no longer adventurous. The aeroplane was another matter, for its mastery demanded not only money but nerve and a lightness of heart not needed for a motoring holiday in the De Dion; nor was its manufacture likely to be as profitable as building motor-cars. Flying and France seemed to go hand in hand. The names of aeroplane components – nacelle, aileron, fuselage, longeron and half a hundred others – were all taken from its language and some still remain. The Wrights apart, all the big names of the first days are those of Frenchmen; Paulhan, Morane, Voisin, Farman, Deperdussin, Hamel, Pegoud and, above all, Bleriot. Their money had to be got where they could find it, for governments could not be expected to use public funds for something that might prove no more than a passing craze. Bleriot earned his from the manufacture of an ingenious car headlamp, and for most of them, prize money put up by newspapers for the first opportunity to perform some feat or other came in handy. Probably the most influential man at the beginning was a non-flier, M. Levauasseur, who had produced a 24 hp engine – named Antoinette, in tactful tribute to the daughter of his backer M. Gastambide. The Antoinette engine won motor-cycle and motor-boat races, as well as propelling M. Santos-Dumont's airship, before it was adapted to power the first successful flying-machines in Europe.

Britain was slower off the mark and it was not until the shadow of Louis Bleriot flitted over Dover Castle in July 1909 that such names as Geoffrey de Haviland, A. V. Roe, Charles Stewart Rolls and Hubert Latham began to appear in print. Most of them flew French machines, or machines powered by French engines, until their own designs began to appear. The story of British aviation during the few years before the Great War is a fascinating one, the men concerned being quite as fascinating as their achievements. In a quieter, less crowded and less regulated England they were allowed to get on with things in their own fashion; if it amused them to risk their money and break their necks it was nobody's business but their own. A benevolent and quite unofficial government lay with the Royal Aero Club, ruling by its prestige as the Alpine Club ruled mountaineering. Until well into the war it was the Club alone that could grant a pilot the right to display the prized insignia of wings. Soldier, sailor and civilian met there to exchange information and had no Royal Aero Club existed there might well have been no RFC in 1914.

All this is well known, and there is a tendency to take the achievements of some other countries more lightly than they deserve. In America Glenn H. Curtiss – one of the few names that still survive in the aircraft industry – flew down the Hudson River from Albany to New York in 1909 in just over two and a half hours. Germany was believed to be lagging behind, interested only in Zeppelins for the Navy, but in 1914 it was German pilots flying German aeroplanes who held the most worthwhile records. From the Zeppelin had also come a bonus: the ability to make engines measuring their horse-power in hundreds rather than in tens. This was to give Germany a long start in the war to come. Russia, as usual, was uncommunicative but her efforts were far from contemptible. Lieutenant Negorof looped the loop before M. Pegoud managed to do the same thing, and the great Sikorsky aeroplane of 1914 with its four engines and a glassed-in fuselage of about the size and shape of a London tram slung between great wings was far in advance of anything else in the world.

It was not until about 1910 that the British War Office began to interest itself in flying, and then only because public opinion was becoming hard to resist. The Royal Navy, never greatly concerned with the weapons of weaker powers, did not reckon much to the Zeppelin; submarines were far more worrying. The Army saw the future of aeroplanes as superior kite-balloons, useful for doing cavalry reconnaissance work and for artillery-spotting. For these purposes a machine was needed that was stable and not too fast; it need carry no armament, for flying was quite dangerous enough without rival airmen making it even more so. Men with longer vision ignored this, and the Royal Aircraft Factory at Farnborough produced, before the war, the best fighting aeroplane, the SE4. It never went into production, and when the Fokker E1V appeared in 1915 there was nothing that could stand against it.

We have come to accept that men who do their fighting in the air are of a breed apart from others, and in this there is truth. To one man nothing could be more horrifying than to be carried into battle inside a coffin of silver spruce poles held together by "doped" linen, at the mercy of a not-too-reliable engine, fighting it out high above the ground with the stability of a fencer on skates and encouraged by the thought that one speck of dirt in the carburettor, one instant of misjudgment or a stroke of sheer misfortune might leave him not merely shot but pulped and roasted. To another, the worst way of spending a war must be to huddle cold, hungry, wet, verminous and bored in a stinking trench, rocked by shells, poisoned by gas, sniped at every moment, cheered by the thought that this was his night to crawl round enemy positions in the dark and waking every morning to the first conscious thought that thus he must continue to exist until a bullet appeared with his name on it. It is pleasant to go into battle wearing a clean shirt, but against that it is something to know that if one falls it can only be to measure one's own length. Why, given the choice, does one man elect for the high road and another for the low?

The handful of Regulars that made up both wings of the Royal Flying Corps in 1914 had made their choice, even though much of what it would mean was hidden from them. Many others had no choice at all. Basil Barrington-Kennett, first Adjutant of the RFC and the man who taught it the blessings of discipline, returned to the Grenadier Guards when their officer casualties had become grievous and died with them at Festubert. Many, like him, felt their old Regiments to have first call and either left flying prematurely or never started. What manner of men were they who brought the strength of the RFC in four years from a few hundreds to nearly a third of a million?

Certainly no one type of flying-recruit emerges. The very large number of hyphenated names amongst the pilots suggests backgrounds of comfort and the suffix RFC appears regularly on the Rolls of Honour in our public schools. It was their function to produce leaders, and right well they did it; if one must select an exemplar it has to be Arthur Rhys-Davids. The grammar schools came close behind, as one would expect, and their paragon is Albert Ball. The biggest killers of all, however, came from neither of these sources. Jimmy McCudden was the complete professional who rose from the ranks on merit; Mick Mannock was a working-class lad with a bent for machinery, an inflexible will and a hatred for the enemy shared by few. Canada produced fine fighter pilots; out of many names Bishop, Collishaw, Barker and Andrew McKeevor must stand out. Australia introduced its own style, for Australians were the great masters of trap and snare. If a lame-looking two-seater were jumped by a German pilot and he in turn was jumped out of the sun by machines with red-white-and-blue roundels, it was long odds that there were Australian pilots in them; this was only the simplest of their many ploys. New Zealand and South Africa supplied high-quality fliers, in number out of all proportion to their small populations, and amongst the Rhodesians was a young man known today as Air Chief Marshal Sir Arthur Harris. American pilots, some under British and some under their own colours, were well on the way into the big league when the Armistice cut them short. Attempts to find clues as to the making of a pilot on the basis of his home country lead nowhere.

Achievement of "ace" stature had to depend on the quality of the training a man received almost as much as upon his personal aptitude. At the beginning of the war and for a long time to come instruction was crude and inadequate, for the machines available were poor and some instructors confined their thoughts to retaining cosy jobs. Many of the young men sent out in 1915 who should have been the flight and squadron leaders of 1918 were killed before they had logged a score of flying hours. Only after Smith-Barry had been given his head did his Gosport System put flying training on a sound footing with dual-controlled aircraft and a speaking-tube to allow conversation between instructor and pupil. He was worth more to the RFC than any "ace".

That there is an airman-type as there is a seaman-type is plain to see; it transcends nationality and class but it is not to be glibly explained. Somewhere, buried deep in every man, lies the cumulative effect of countless generations of different ancestors. Either it makes him by temperament a flier, or it does not. As the Army used to say, "There is black, and there is white. There are no shades of grey." The infantry subaltern on the ground might catch the eye of the Flying Corps subaltern in the air and each might say firmly, "Thank God I do not have his job".

By the summer of 1918 the RAF had complete air superiority. Looking back cold-bloodedly after two generations one can make a case for saying that it was a pity that victory came so soon afterwards. New aircraft, the Dolphin, Snipe, Hippo and Salamander, streets ahead of anything that had gone before, were coming into service, including the first armoured aeroplane designed for ground-strafing. Had Plan 1919 ever been put into effect these would have combined with the Mark VIII tank, better by far than any the Army had in 1939, the armoured troop-carrier and the swift tanklets built to operate far in advance of the battle line in raiding headquarters and disrupting communications. The Independent Air Force, with its great Handley-Page 0/400s and V1500s, stood ready and able to bomb Berlin. Germany would have been over-run and German eyes would have seen the falsity of assertions that the German Army had never been squarely beaten in the field. No doubt American formations would have been needed in an Army of Occupation to save the country from Bolshevism and the Great Republic could hardly have withdrawn from the world. Lance-Corporal Hitler, A., could have taken his honourable discharge, became a passable painter and decorator, and the twentieth century would have been spared a second blitzkrieg twenty years later.

When the RFC merged into the RAF in April 1918 it had already begotten strong sons. Billy Hughes had insisted on forming a national flying service for Australia; his namesake Sam was on the point of doing the same thing for Canada when the end came. The United States Air Force would not disdain kinship. When America came into the war she had nothing more formidable than her WAC0 and JN4 trainers to put into the air. With magnanimity President Wilson allowed his young men to become attached to the going concern and the mixture of khaki and olive-drab in Messes and on airfields worked splendidly. Fifteen thousand US mechanics serviced RFC engines and very welcome they were. Two squadrons, Nos. 17 and 148, both flying Camels, were all-American and names like Sam Eckert, Mort Newhall, Bim Oliver, George Vaughn and Alex Matthews were amongst the most popular and respected in the business. Those of Luke, Lufbery and Rickenbacker are amongst the immortals. On the strength of this I have allowed myself one lapse into the Second World War. Jimmy Doolittle was a 1917 pilot but had the misfortune to be denied the chance of showing his mettle during the first round. When his country was staggering under a coward's blow in the solar plexus, "Jimmy Doolittle's Raid" was exactly what America needed. Since greater events soon overtook it there is danger that it may slip men's memories and that would be a great pity.

A short note on the use of the term "ace" seems necessary. It is, of course, a straight translation from the French "as", a nearly-official award to a pilot who had destroyed five or more enemy aircraft. If any British pilot ever used it there would have been heavy irony in the word, for it was detested by everybody. A French "ace" was encouraged to show off in public because it was reckoned good for morale. Something of the same kind happened in Germany. The British view of the matter was simple. In the first place any attempt to run a kind of league table for gallantry is indecent. In the second, it is futile. How do you rank a middle-aged observer who has flown for weary years in a slow two-seater far over the enemy lines, looking minutely at the ground, evaluating what he sees and noting it down, taking careful photographs, changing plates though he can hardly move his hands for cold and, in his spare time, keeping watch around and behind for the fighter against which he and his pilot have practically no defence? Does he come above or below the bright-eyed youth who in a few weeks strikes down half a dozen men like him? The whole business is an absurdity, though newspapers loved it. After the war Bishop became very angry indeed when rival papers ran a private battle over whether or not he had scored more than Mannock. Mannock, had he lived, would have visited their offices with a stick. Remember also that the big scores were mostly made at the end of the war when the air was full of machines. A pilot of 1915 who had shot down one or two was quite a figure; even Immelmann claimed only fifteen. To stand high in the averages it was necessary either to survive the early years by some means or to have come in late.

The characters in this book are not necessarily the top scorers; some, on the strict definition, do not qualify as "aces" at all. I have taken them, not at random, because all are, to me at any rate, interesting. If there were to be a batting order space would have had to be found for Raymond Collishaw with sixty-eight, Philip Fullard with fifty-three – both more than Ball – Beauchamp-Proctor and Andrew McKeevor, who on two occasions shot down three in a day. The list is long, but nobody would wish for a score-book.

On the summit, beyond challenge, stands the biggest destroyer of all. The Aircraft Disposal Co. Ltd., between the summer of 1919 and the spring of 1920, sold the Royal Air Force – all 10,000 machines and spares almost beyond counting – for £5,700,000. Nearly all of it went for scrap.

CHAPTER ONE

D'Artagnan With Wings

Robert Loraine

Actors, taken as a whole, are not reputed men of outstanding valour, for it is unreasonable to expect heroism on stage to spill over into life. When Captain Radford, alias Gilbert the Filbert the Kernel of the Knuts or Basil Hallam, fell to a dreadful death from a balloon over the Somme there was a moment of incredulity before he received the honour due to his memory. He was not the only member of the profession to win fame far from the footlights.

Robert Loraine was born to the stage and is best remembered on both sides of the Atlantic as an actor. To him this was a secondary matter. In the autumn of 1899 he was playing D'Artagnan against Tree's Athos at His Majesty's and was plainly on his way to the top, but the moment war came in South Africa he threw it all away and fell in behind the drum. Trooper Loraine of the Montgomeryshire Yeomanry belied his almost indecently handsome appearance; he had been very hard up in youth, working as a stevedore in Liverpool and earning an honest copper giving dramatic recitals in sailors' dives, in consequence of which he was a very tough young man. He became a skilled horseman, an expert with the Colt machine-gun and saw as much fighting against the elusive Boer as did any other "Yeoboy".

By spring 1901 the pitched battles were over and his engagement was running out. There had been plenty of time during intervals of boredom to keep up a correspondence with useful people and when an offer came from Charles Frohman to perform in New York he jumped at it. The play, *To Have and to Hold*, was a poor rewrite of Mary Johnson's *By Order of the Company*, fine swashbuckling stuff, but it did not last long. Robert's good looks, however, captivated the female part of the audience and he was instantly taken on in a musical comedy winsomely called *Frocks and Frills* in which he played an English peer known as "Beautiful Bob". He loathed the part but it paid well and, as his widow ambiguously put it, "he had a large woman following". To this Robert had not the smallest objection, and he spent like an oil sheikh on holiday. It could not be for long; disgust with a reputation he did not want soon set in and Robert returned home to play Henry V. The money was far less but he did not much mind. Other actors may have played the victor of Agincourt better but none ever felt more at one with him. The money evaporated and he had returned to New York for two more plays when he had a stroke of good fortune. George Bernard Shaw, after a quarrel with his American agent, sold Robert the rights for performances in the States of *Man and Superman* for £200. The play opened in New York late in 1905, and was followed by a triumphant tour of America and its place was taken with equal success by *Arms and the Man*. From these Robert made a considerable fortune.

It was Shaw who introduced him to the air. On a day in 1907 the Irishman, desiring better acquaintance with gas-bags, hired a balloon and invited the young actor to join him, Mrs. Shaw and Harley Granville Barker in a flight from Wandsworth Gas-works. They floated over north Kent as far as Cobham Common and Robert was captivated. Balloons were all very well, but what he now wanted was a flying-machine. Next year, breaking away from his part as a proto-Jeeves gentleman's gentleman at the Haymarket Theatre, he went to Issy-les-Moulineaux and watched entranced as Henri Farman

got his flying bedstead six feet into the air, made an uncertain
circuit and came down unscathed. Robert at once ordered a
similar machine but the queue was long and it never arrived.
In the following July he attended on Louis Bleriot at Sangatte,
making a nuisance of himself by continually striking matches
in the open to persuade Bleriot of the clemency of the weather.
It was to Robert that Bleriot handed his crutches – he had
burnt his feet in a recent crash – when he soared into immortal-
ity. Robert demanded that a more powerful machine, fit to
carry a passenger, be instantly made for him.

In 1909 no engine of sufficient power for this purpose existed
and Bleriot suggested that whilst experiment continued Robert
should enrol as a pupil at his Pau school. By now Robert was
playing Young Marlow in *She Stoops to Conquer* and his life was
spent dashing from the Haymarket to Victoria en route for Pau
and back again. Instruction was not refined. "The pupil is
pitched into the seat and briefly shown how to work the controls, and the use of the throttle and switch. His machine is
then given a push and he is turned loose with orders to drive
about on his wheels until he can steer her straight. In order that
he shall not blunder inadvertently into the air, the central
lever, otherwise the cloche or joy-stick, is tied well forward. So
he rushes round like a decapitated chicken until he flops sideways with one wing-tip broken; which is precisely what happened to me this morning." He was expected to repeat all but
the last part of this evolution every day for some weeks, when
the cord would be removed and the pupil permitted to make a
flight round the aerodrome. Robert, granted only six days'
leave, would have none of that. On the third day he surreptiti-
ously undid the string, opened the throttle wide and raced
along the ground. When flat out, he pulled the cloche experi-
mentally back hoping to become airborne. Nothing happened.
"I was greatly puzzled. Then it occurred to me that the engine
might lack power." It probably did, for Bleriot knew his man.
"Next day I was at the school before dawn to bribe the
mechanic in charge to let me have a less used-up engine for my
practice. In this I was successful." He was also probably less

than candid. "Again I went to the far corner of the field and untied the cloche and opened the throttle all out, to find that the new engine gave me much more power. So, as soon as I had full speed on, I pulled back the cloche with great determination and we leapt into the air. At last I was flying! I, myself, alone. I was fulfilling an instinct so strong that it easily over-rode any other instinct of self-preservation. I looked at the ground and felt like a conqueror. I looked at the sky and wanted more. More of this exaltation. Altitude, height, height. Nothing simpler. I pulled back the cloche. The machine leapt higher, so did my heart, higher still – then – paff – I came to earth, having stalled and crashed. As I picked myself out of the debris, somewhat dazed by a gash on the forehead, I realized that I must cultivate a lighter hand on the joystick. All the same, I was very happy." Bleriot was not; the cost of repair fell on him and he refused to provide any more aeroplanes. Young Marlow appeared for some time with a bandage under his white wig.

As relations with Bleriot could never be quite the same again, Robert took himelf back to Henri Farman to see what he could buy off the peg. He settled for a biplane, cruder by far than any of Bleriot's monoplanes; it had no fuselage, the pilot being perched on a plank in the open, and looked more like an insect than an aeroplane, but it had one compensating advantage. The 50 hp Gnome rotary engine was twice as powerful as any of the Anzani radials fitted to the other machines and was reckoned the last word so far in performance. True, it had but one valve and the lubrication was on the lines of a two-stroke motor lawnmower but the pretty blue haze made by the castor oil was behind the pilot and would lose itself in the air. He paid the £7,000 demanded without a murmur, and also seduced away Farman's top mechanic, M. Vedrines, with an offer of £150 a month.

Vedrines was the perfect foil to Loraine. He was, and not merely in his own opinion, the best man in the business and a Gascon who made a perfect Planchet to his patron's D'Artagnan. Soon he learnt that he was going to earn his huge salary.

Whatever Robert wanted, however impossible or absurd, Robert must have; and at once. Vedrines left his own account of the matter in his memoirs. After observing that only in England could an actor even want to fly – "imagine Guitry, Monet, Sully or Jean Bloch leaving the stage, their parts and make-up to pilot an aeroplane" – he spoke of his employer. "Loraine was brave, cool and possessed of a remarkable decision, but he had the soul of a poet; and a poet does not make a reliable pilot. So, even though Loraine was the most enterprising pilot I have ever known, he was never a good one . . . and oh! – what a dose he gave me of continual foolhardiness."

It was necessary for Robert to take his pilot's brevet. The coolness between him and Bleriot was worse than that *vis-à-vis* Farman and it was to the Farman school that he went to be examined. The test demanded two figures-of-eight, three landings within twenty yards of a mark, an ascent to 400 feet followed by the cutting out of the engine at 100 and a volplané to earth with the same twenty-yard margin of error. Robert, having cracked up every biplane there – or so Vedrines said – managed to pass in an unusually short time. With his brevet safe in his pocket he entered his own Farman Racer for the Bournemouth July Meeting. In the meantime he took it in pieces to Beaulieu where he intended to put in some flying time in preparation.

The English aviators of 1910 made up a very close borough, and Loraine was not a member. The well-known names – to the public some were very well known – included, amongst the fliers, Charles Stewart Rolls, J. T. C. Moore-Brabazon, Claude Grahame-White, James Radley and Graham Gilmour; of designers the best known were Geoffrey de Havilland, a professional engineer who had come into flying after designing London buses, and A. V. Roe, late of the Merchant Navy, whose tiny firm was kept up by the profits of the family factory making Bullseye Braces for the trousers of working men. Few of them had any money and what they did have went into their aeroplanes. Brooklands motor racing ground was their home and many of them pigged it happily in odd corners of their sheds.

Their relationships were cordial, their social centre a hut called the Blue Bird where a committee of equally dedicated wives dispensed refreshment, and they could not be expected to welcome a wealthy actor who would inevitably be suspected of trifling with their darling schemes. Robert sensibly adopted a *nom-de-vol*; the pilot of the Farman appeared inconspicuously as "Mr. Jones". He too was dedicated and scorned to use his flying as a publicity stunt.

Because aeroplanes cost a great deal of money their owners were naturally chary about flying them in other than the finest of weather. Robert, secure in a large bank balance, affected to find in this a sign of pusillanimity and set himself to go out daily no matter what the barometer said. *Man and Superman* had brought him in some £40,000 and he could afford to take risks. "I found that flying in gusty winds was more alarming than dangerous and that rain made flying difficult but not, as was believed at the time, impossible".

On the day before the Bournemouth July Meeting Robert came down heavily and damaged his machine. Vedrines announced himself unable to repair it without screws of a kind unprocurable in Beaulieu village. Robert, with unkind words, sent him off to the undertaker to buy coffin screws. Vedrines was horrified, burst into tears and announced, "C'est que j'ai affreusement la nostalgie. Dieu, que j'ai mal du pays." (I feel homesick. God, do I feel homesick.") He never really liked England. The coffin screws, however, were bought and Robert on his racer rose into a sky of grey cotton wool.

George Smart, an old friend who combined love for both aviation and the theatre, had charge of the Bournemouth end of affairs. For hours he hung about waiting for Robert but no news came in. Late that night he arrived at the hotel, in a filthy temper but lacking an aeroplane. It was, apparently, somewhere in a wood and in many pieces. Six farm carts brought them to the hangar next day; Vedrines, told to re-build it at once, mutinied. Offers of money were in vain. The Gascon went for a walk to demonstrate his severance of relations and there he met Bleriot and Morane. He told of his troubles;

Bleriot said something wounding about the Gascon's professional ability. He could not have done Robert a better service. The affronted Vedrines stalked back to the hangar, surveyed the wreckage and gabbled a list of his requirements. Robert got instantly in touch with the Farman works with details of necessary replacements; Henri Farman paid him out for luring away his mechanic by jacking up all the prices, but he did deliver. The bill came to nearly £1,000.

The brotherhood of fliers, most of whom had brought their machines to Bournemouth in crates, found Mr. Jones the best joke they had come across for years. Presumably none of them were theatre-goers for nobody connected him with Robert Loraine, one of the best-known actors of the day. If Bleriot knew, he very decently kept his mouth shut.

Vedrines, reasonably enough, demanded assistance. Robert, who spared nobody once his mind was made up, scoured the country and managed to muster a force of twenty craftsmen, most of them hired in London at vast wages on condition that they lived on the job and were game to work at all hours. "Hammer Hangar", named by reason of its incessant noise, became notorious and it fell to Smart to keep the peace between Vedrines and his xenophobic assistants. It was not the easiest of jobs; had the workmen understood even a fraction of what Vedrines had to say to them they would have walked off no matter how high the pay. They ate where they stood, slept in their clothes and by degrees the pile of rubbish once again became an aeroplane. Robert's part was that of the galley-slave overseer in Ben Hur; he got away with it partly through lavish expenditure but more because his determination was infectious.

The day of the race dawned to reveal an aerodrome with all its flags at half-mast, for Charles Stewart Rolls – the Rolls of Rolls-Royce – had crashed to his death the day before. He, more than any other man, had been the leader and the loss was bitter. Loraine was amongst the first on the scene and noticed that "his face as I saw him lying in the wreckage a moment after his fall showed nothing but a calm content". He had not been the only casualty at the Meeting – Robert's neighbour, Rawlinson, had been terribly injured as a result of bad repair work to his machine – and it took courage to carry on as if nothing had happened. Robert did not see it as a warning. "The outburst (by anti-aviationists) made me keener than ever to prove how wrong were the blind fools who condemned aviation as an idle break-neck hobby and failed to see in this development the highway of the future."

Out of respect for Rolls the race was postponed until noon and as the hours dragged by the beautiful morning began to give way to leaden skies and a strong, gusty wind. Robert sat on rather than in his aeroplane brushing away not only stewards but men of the calibre of Cody, Morane and Dixon all of whom entreated him not to take off in the face of the approaching storm. He would have none of it. His faith in Vedrines was complete and, as Smart recorded, "he had fretted and fumed and literally cried because his machine could not be re-built in a day. Now he was ready, and what did the appeals of friends or the admonitions of the winds of Heaven signify? Robert, up to that moment, had been a nonentity. A condition of things too intolerable to be borne." His only words were to Vedrines. "Lancez l'helice."

The engine sprang to life, helpers clung desperately to the tail which was rapidly becoming invisible through the banks of castor oil fumes. Vedrines stood aside, hand cupped over ear and listening to the note of the engine with all the concentration of a pointer. As soon as he was satisfied with what he heard, a single nod was enough to unleash his master. Robert raised his hand, the Farman staggered forward, losing its acolytes one by one as they fell face downward on the grass. As the machine rose into the air, its ungainliness transformed into grace and beauty, the rain came down and a mist began to cover the horizon. The word "suicide" dominated the conversation of those left behind. A shaft of lightning, instantly followed by an earth-shaking roll of thunder, drove them all under cover as Robert was swallowed up by an inky cloud. Vedrines, in the sympathetic company of Bleriot and Morane, keened loudly on the theme that no machine, not even one built by Vedrines, could survive such a tempest.

Invisible to them all, Loraine was ploughing doggedly on, one hand on the stick and the other gripping for dear life the plank which made his only support. Within a minute he was soaked to the skin, his leather jacket and life-saving waistcoat sodden and dripping. Since he carried no instruments of any kind he could only keep heading for the Needles by guesswork; an attempt to climb above the storm failed, for the engine showed signs of faltering and leaving him with the dreaded cabré, the backward fall that had killed so many of the early flying men. Once he returned to the level it picked up again but there was nothing for him to see but rain, pouring in sheets over the wings and splashing back from them over the valiant Gnome which was roaring its little heart out. "Presently, because I could not see, I lost all sense of gravity. I could not tell whether the earth was under me, to the right of me or to the left of me. Whether I was flying slantwise or straight, I was utterly lost in the dark. I had to balance the machine by guesswork after each buffeting had all but pitched me out of my seat. My watch stopped, so I had no means of gauging the petrol expenditure, but the blind pitching in the rain and cloud seemed to have gone on for hours, so I had a nasty feeling the petrol would soon be giving out." He had, in fact, been blown far out over the Channel, well beyond the Isle of Wight, but had by some instinct managed to make a turn back in the right direction. Suddenly a break came in the clouds through which he saw a patch of green to the left some 1,500 feet below, just at the moment when he was finally giving up hope. In his excitement he dived for it like a striking gannet until the wings began to protest; he flattened out, having lost visibility again, when a mighty puff of wind seized him and threw him up like a cork on a breaker. The aeroplane was flying straight into a cliff and without this providential blast he would have smashed into it and added the name of Jones to that of Rolls and the others. As it was, the machine was lifted and set down on the cliff top, "on a thirty yard strip of table-land surrounded on all but one side by a sheer fall of rock many hundred feet to the sea". At that moment the sun chose to come out, the storm clouds disappeared and Robert found himself perched on the 18th green of the golf links above Alum Bay. Vedrines arrived by motor-boat and his greeting was not congratulatory. "Quite an original idea. Altogether novel for an aeroplane to land like this on a seagull's perch. I see that, as usual, you have given no thought to the machine." A party of gunners dragged the aeroplane into the safety of a nearby chalk-pit while the farmer whose land it was promptly put up a barrier and charged spectators threepence a head to look at it. The pilot solemnly put his name to many autograph books as "Robert Jones". He knew himself to be the hero of the moment but had no intention of cashing in on a brief fame. Flying was far more important to Robert Loraine than the theatre, which served only to provide the bread, butter and coffin screws. Not many men would have passed up such an opportunity to advertise themselves. He allowed himself to be dried out and went straight home to London.

Four days later Robert came back for the return flight; it was plain to those who knew him best that something had happened during the interval, for he showed a marked reluctance to take off even on a day of high summer. Only Vedrines understood what was ailing him. The terrible experience of the outward flight had shaken Loraine more than he had realized and he was on the point of losing his nerve at the sight of the abyss which he must cross at the moment of becoming airborne. Vedrines, in his own way, was no bad psychologist. It would be futile to try working on Robert's own emotions for he was not one to be much influenced by the opinions of others, and Vedrines had a better way. He accused the patron not of funk but of a sad lack of confidence in the work of his mechanic, adding for good measure that were Loraine to find an excuse for refusing to fly he would turn every man in the crowd into an anti-aviationist. It was enough. Robert clenched his teeth, climbed aboard and took off straight over the cliff edge. He never did a braver thing; the return journey was easy and on arrival at Bournemouth he was his own man once more. Vedrines was generous. "Ah, le beau geste. How truly he always had the cause of flying at heart. And at that moment I forgave him all his troublesome idiosyncracies. What a man he was to serve; always he pulled the long nose at fear. Bravo Loraine."

The company moved on to the next meeting, at Blackpool. The show there was purely a commercial business, depending for its profits on beer and shrimps, the business of the aviators being to amuse and thus to pull the crowds. None of them much cared for this but there were handsome prizes to be won and most of them needed the money. For the promoters it was Grahame-White's show. He was the best stunt pilot in the business and could be trusted to give value. Robert, short-sighted and clumsy, knew himself to be no match for such a gladiator in the way of circus tricks and had no intention of competing with "Claudie" in this way. He had a private plan of his own. On August Bank Holiday morning the Farman looked at its most beautiful, for Vedrines had insisted on the addition of his brother Jules, "de luxe" carpenter, who had arrived two days earlier accompanied by two expensive-looking Frenchwomen of undetermined status. He it was who had varnished spars and planes to a brightness never before seen, as if for a *concours d'elegance*. Mr. Jones entered the Time in Air competition, for the flier who remained longest aloft without counting descents for re-fuelling. He took off in blazing sunshine and, instead of beginning a series of long circuits over the aerodrome, sailed away southwards towards the sea. The other pilots, Grahame-White, A. V. Roe, Tetard, Chavez and the rest, dutifully amused the paying public by flying round and round cutting figures of eight. Robert had disappeared and nobody bothered about him. Then came a bellow over a megaphone. "Jones is now flying over Liverpool." Grahame-White was forgotten as more and more messages came in over the roar of engines. "Jones has flown over the Mersey", Jones has passed over Birkenhead" and finally "Jones has had engine trouble and has come down on a sand-bank in the Ribble. The tide is rising and there is a channel between the sandbank and the mainland." Jones seemed in serious danger; this was well worth a shilling, better value by far than boring circuits. Disappointment was bravely hidden when news came in that Robert was quite safe, not in the Ribble but on a firm piece of mainland, once more hard by a golf course where he was having tea. The Vedrines, Smart and Gibbs the chauffeur drove as fast as they dared to the spot and finished such work as was needed just in time for the Farman to rise up again into the sunset, the last rays turning its wings first to copper and then to gold. The organizers tried to twist Robert out of his prize because he had kept out of sight but they knew only the shadowy Jones and not the substantial Loraine. Robert spoke to them very roughly and they agreed that the prize should be his if he would just amuse the crowd for a quarter of an hour. He did. It was the worst piece of deliberately sloppy flying ever seen at such a meeting. The judges had to admit that he had been in the air for two and a quarter hours; the nearest rival had endured only one and a half but he had been the better entertainer. Robert got the second prize of £50. He spent it on their dinner.

The summer of 1910 was hard on Loraine's understudy as Charles Surface in *The School for Scandal,* Tree's production at His Majesty's Theatre which was playing to well-attended houses, for he spent far more time rehearsing with the Vedrines menage than at his legitimate performances. Beerbohm Tree was not the mildest of men nor is it likely that the future of aviation bulked large in his thoughts. He seems to have behaved with creditable restraint, especially when no publicity was forthcoming from all these extra-mural activities. When the meeting ended Robert bribed one of the stewards to leave his hangar standing for he had more plans of his own.

Rolls had flown across the Channel and back but nobody had yet tackled the Irish Sea. Flying over water was still reckoned a hazardous business and with every justification. Robert, born and educated in New Brighton, knew the Lancashire coastline pretty well and was determined to have a try at it. Early in the morning of 10 August the Gnome sang its *aubade* satisfactorily into Vedrines' cupped ear and Robert sailed away once more to the south. The weather was fine and a bank of early mist rising to about 400 feet did not worry him, for the Farman could easily climb above that. It did, but once the cloud was underfoot Robert found himself unable to stop his ascent. Only by applying brute force to the elevator control could he make the Farman return to something like level flight, avoiding the risk of the dreaded cabré, but the effect was to bend the lever like a bow and set up a vibration throughout the whole machine which was hardly less alarming. Robert spotted the cause at once. Vedrines had apparently permitted his brother, the *charpentier-de-luxe*, to rise above his station and adjust the angle of incidence of the planes. They were now set firmly with the leading edges far too high and nothing could be done about it. "I was on the point of turning back, for my right arm was becoming numbed by the effort necessary to hold the plane on a level course, when a panorama of such loveliness unfurled before me in the long range of Snowdon's mountains winking before me like diamonds above an opal mist that I could no more have turned my back on them than a true believer on Paradise." Vedrines was right to call Robert a poet. D'Artagnan would have felt exactly the same way. "Entranced I flew on, exalted, until I was about to hit yellow sands again, where the peninsula of the Great Orme heads out to the sea. Looking down, I also caught sight of my watch, and saw that I had been up an hour and a half. Well, petrol would not last for ever and I happened to be over a golf course. I had to descend. The question was, would the elevator control lever stand the strain of being bent yet farther over or snap? Indeed, could my numbed arm bend it over at all? I strained and strained; at last it moved over and nothing snapped. The sweat was pouring off me as I switched off the current and immediately a swifter rush of air began whistling past my head as the earth dashed up to meet me. At 300 feet I switched on again and eased up, selected a spot free of bunkers and, turning towards it, cut off and came down on a fairway that gleamed like an emerald – came down so gently that not a daisy was bruised. Decidedly Vedrines would say my landings were improving." A man in pyjamas, waving a toothbrush, ran out from the clubhouse and told Loraine that he was creating a hazard at the Rhos-on-Sea links. Had the royal and ancient game never been invented, flying in 1910 would hardly have been possible.

By 3.00 p.m. the team had arrived. Vedrines did what was necessary, had a conversation with his brother mercifully unintelligible to others, and at 4.30 Robert was ready to take off again. The crowd would have none of it and refused to budge. For two and a half hours Robert sat on his plank smoking cigarette after cigarette until the unlikely alliance of a Boy Scout troop and a company of pierrots commanded by the club secretary cleared the way. The take-off was difficult, demanding a sudden rocketing up in order to clear telegraph wires, but Robert managed it. The long wait had unsettled him and by flying directly into the sunset he soon lost his way. "There was no sign of land, not a ship in sight to break the solitude, only unreal water which glistened here and there where the heat haze did not obscure it. The compass tied to my left-hand strut was useless owing to the vibration of my engine and the deviation caused by the magneto. Where was I? I had no instruments to tell me what my course should by. My wrist-watch told me that my petrol tank was half empty. I felt rather a fool and that I was justifying the many accusations against me of recklessness. Where could I be?" Doing the only sensible thing, he climbed in order to enlarge his vision. Once higher up, he saw land; it was not the land he expected, the coast of Anglesey, but the Calf of Man, and that away to the north-east. He swung the plane away, keeping the sunset over his right shoulder, and headed in the general direction of Anglesey where he was expected. After losing sight even of the Calf and while meditating that "I did feel rather like a Thomlinson shrieking through space" he was suddenly heartened by something below about the size and shape of a tea-tray. It was Anglesey right enough but the sight of it coincided with an expiring cough from the Gnome indicating the end of his petrol. "My engine stopped about a mile from shore, but I was high

enough to glide to land, and so I made my first volplané."
At 1.00 a.m. Robert arrived at the Station Hotel, Holyhead,
in a farm cart, well pleased with himself. "A perfect atteris-
age," he observed gravely, "in a field sixteen miles from
here."

Almost at once the weather broke. Rain and gales whipped
North Wales. Vedrines was again in tears because a passing
pig had eaten the bucketful of extra-special varnish he had
prepared for the anointment of the wings during the last and
longest stage. A farmer's wife who spoke nothing but Welsh
collaborated with him in brewing an acceptable substitute in
her copper. Robert had a brief sleep and emerged at 5.00 a.m.,
to find a wind gusting up to 40 mph. The usual entreaties met
with the usual blank wall. The Farman left the ground with a
following wind, wavered for about a hundred yards and
crashed into the side of a small hill. Robert quitted his plank
just in time to avoid injury. Once more his aeroplane had
become a mess of torn canvas and shattered wood. The
weather, apparently satisfied, instantly became summer again.
Robert, ever the actor, filled and lit a pipe. His only comment
was, "It was the wind. I could feel it pushing me down."

It is kindest to say least about the next three weeks. The
Vedrines *frères* demanded that the ladies who might have been
their wives be brought over to help in accordance with their
talents. Robert agreed. The *charpentier-de-luxe* proved useless
and Robert tried to sack him. A common front was at once
formed. Happily the matter resolved itself. On a certain night
one of the ladies spoke slightingly to the other about the
relative merits of their escorts, who promptly set about each
other with knives. In the morning Vedrines was able to tell *le
patron* that Jules had departed with his lady friend and that
serious work could now begin. Such a moment brought out the
best in the Gascon and on 5 September the Farman was,
incredibly, ready to take the air again. All that remained of the
original was the engine. The work had been done in a Welsh
bog, completely in the open and in the face of every difficulty
made by a bloody-minded farmer out to screw every penny he

could from Robert's misfortune. Vedrines was, indeed, the best man in the business. The tugs had been cancelled, a better compass of the oil variety made to strap on the pilot's knee and all was ready.

The engine was started, the Farman trundled forward. Before it had got far there came a loud explosion and it came to rest stuck in the bog. Robert's legs were pinned under the mainplane boom which carried the weight of the engine. When they got him out he could not stand but examination showed only bruises and sprains. Nobody had realized the earth to be a mere crust with a morass underneath it. Though Robert was lucky to be alive he still had his difficulties. In a week's time he was due to open in Ibsen's *The Man from the Sea* and his mood exactly matched that of the author's cheerless hero. After a moment of self-examination he decided to continue. Smart arranged with Lord Sheffield for the use of a field at Penrhos Park and thence the Farman was ignominiously dragged by road.

On the following Sunday Robert took his place again. He looked little like Beautiful Bob, in two sweaters, a padded waistcoat and a patent jacket of reindeer hide warranted to keep him afloat for five days. Lest this be unreliable, a lifeboatman's cork belt was superimposed over all and he was just about capable of movement. The take-off was unremarkable and, with a following wind from the east, he began the journey in fine style. The Farman rose to 4,000 feet; then the engine stopped. Feeling violently sick as the sea rushed up to meet him, Loraine retained his presence of mind. The only part of the engine subject to his control was the petrol supply and there was a sporting chance that this was the cause of the trouble. He fiddled furiously with the tap, trying to get fuel flowing again without over-choking, half his mind wondering whether sea would be as unyielding as asphalt. Then, with only twenty feet to go, the Gnome made a spluttering noise and burst into song. Robert flew warily on the level for a bit and then dared a climb. As soon as he reached a decent height, the same thing happened again. In all the mischief repeated itself five times; the reason was later found to be that small pellets of solder in the petrol tank had worked loose and were rolling to and fro across the feed pipe.

The oil-compass at least seemed to be working, though for fifty minutes, when periods of quiet flight permitted, Robert looked in vain for something that was neither sea nor sky. For a while a rain squall kept him occupied in balancing his machine fore and aft and then with its usual suddenness land hove in sight, with the Kish lightship plain to see. A glance at his watch showed that he had covered sixty-four miles – three times Bleriot's flight of a year before – in seventy minutes. The flight was nearly over and Robert felt a strong feeling of *hubris*. Nemesis, as usual, followed. "She began to plunge and dip in the most alarming fashion. Now she would rear up, now she would dive, then she would heel over to the left, then to the right. There was nothing for it but to go on. For at least two minutes we went along heeled over to the right at an angle of 45 degrees. I was certain we were going to slip down sideways, but I got the lever in my left hand and pulled it over as far as it would go and at last she came up again. I was sweating all over in spite of being terribly cold. All the while we were losing altitude fast and, very soon after the trouble began, I saw I was down to some 500 feet. Then I caught a glimpse of Howth Head away to my right and I can tell you I was thankful to see it. It was a terrible job turning her round towards it, but eventually she answered the rudder and we continued our diving and tumbling, losing height in the most alarming fashion. By the time we were within 100 yards of the Head we were down to 100 feet, tossing about worse than ever. There was only one chance. If I could climb another fifty feet I might just manage to land beyond the edge of the lower cliff. The way to do this was to turn her into the wind and trust to her coming up against it. I put her over. For some awful moments I thought she would not take it, but finally she swung round. I had one instant of hope, then something else went. We plunged straight into the sea." At that moment his worst troubles began. Robert sensibly dived as deep as he could in order to clear the wires; in the process his lifebelt shifted and when he broke surface it was with his feet. The cork was keeping them afloat admirably, but his head was six feet under. Somehow he fought himself clear and arrived above water just in time to see his Farman lying on her back with her wheels in the air looking pathetically like a shot duck. Robert swam to the lighthouse where he encountered the final problem. The keeper was determinded to save him; Robert was equally determined not to be saved. If he could not land on Irish soil in his aeroplane he would at least get there unaided. The flight ended with Robert and the lighthouse man standing in the shallows swearing and swinging punches at each other until the aviator was able to escape and climb up the rocks under his own power. He was just two miles short of Dublin. The fact remained he was the first to make the crossing. When Mr. Loraine shook off Mr. Jones and made his entrance for the first night of *The Man from the Sea* the audience never knew how apposite it was. Mr. Jones was seen no more and the Aero Club gave its medal to Robert Loraine. To keep up an incognito now was hopeless.

London was in no mood for lugubrious plays and this one was soon taken off. Thus freed, Robert scrapped the last remains of the salvaged Farman and bought not one but two Bristols in replacement. At the controls of one of these he found his way into the Official History of the Royal Air Force. "During the manoeuvres of 1910 Mr. Robert Loraine in a Bristol machine fitted with transmitting apparatus, succeeded in sending wireless messages, from a distance of a quarter of a mile, to a temporary receiving station rigged up at Larkhill." Soon after that both the new machines were destroyed in a fire.

Vedrines had done well out of Bobby Loraine, though he earned every penny, and he was about to bow out. He observed that the crash off Howth Head had been occasioned by the English wire he had been constrained to use, went to join Bleriot at Pau, was the first to fly the Pyrenees and also got a mention in the Official History. "The wonderful little Delerdussin monoplane, in the 1912 Gordon Bennett Trials at Rheims, carried its pilot, M. Vedrines, at a speed of nearly two miles a minute for a flight of over an hour."

With the loss of both Bristols and the failure of the *Man from the Sea,* Robert was obliged to take stock of his affairs and was reluctantly persuaded that he had spent the whole of his money and more. For the next four years it was all theatre and no flying. By August 1914, not having stinted himself in other respects, he was just about solvent.

When war was declared Loraine instantly formed up to the War Office and was given a Special Reserve commission as a Second Lieutenant in the RFC. At 38 he was probably the oldest subaltern. Maurice Baring was three years his elder but Baring was not a pilot. Loraine arrived at Farnborough and reported himself to Major Trenchard; he was something of a Rip van Winkle, for Trenchard had not made his first flight until after Jones' interment. Robert was invited to refresh himself with a little flying on one of the Maurice Farmans that had been too decrepit even to go to France. He crashed it on landing and demanded another. When he crashed that also, Major Brancker was ordered to break it to him that he was too expensive to be retained. Robert, back in the Henry V role and almost audibly declaiming that now all the middle-age of England is on fire, was so stricken that Trenchard let him go to join a squadron, but only as an observer. He arrived just in time to see the tide turn at the Marne but his exploits spotting for the guns and seeing what the enemy was about were much the same as those of other men. His short-sightedness was not helpful and at least once he was nearly sent home. He did, however, maintain his reputation for bravery out of the common. On 2 November he was observer-gunner in a terrible contraption, a Henri Farman with a seat between the skids immediately underneath the pilot, both in the open as in the old days. Somewhere near Menin the pilot, Moutray-Read, was hit by a shell splinter and blood began to pour down over Robert's head and shoulders. As he had no idea what was happening he climbed out of his perch, made his way over the wing to the pilot and there he stayed until Moutray-Read was able to bring them down. That done, Robert saw him off to hospital and flew the machine away. It was just like old times;

the engine failed after a few miles and Robert force-landed at Dickebusch. A few days later he was in the air again with a like-minded man. Corbett-Wilson had also flown the Irish Sea, two years after Robert, and they stood a little apart from the young men of No. 3 Squadron. At Fromelles there was a rather famous German anti-aircraft battery and on 22 November they decided to tease it. The fact that a strong east wind kept them almost motionless above the gun-site made it all the more fun. To their annoyance the Germans took not the least notice and a vexed Robert dropped them a note. "Keep your eye in. We will be back this afternoon." The next note in his diary, written at Lillers Casualty Clearing Station and dated the following day, says, "At 3.10 p.m. I was shot." He was, yet again, fortunate to live. A bullet had gone through his right lung and out under the collar-bone. Undoubtedly game and set to the German. Twice Robert received the Last Sacrament. More than once the curtains were placed round his bed. He had no intention, however, of dying until the war was won. From a hospital in Park Lane he was sent on a six-week cruise to South America in RMS *Alcantara* in order to get his strength back. On his return, at the height of what was called "the Fokker scourge", he took up promises made by Salmond and Trenchard long ago and was sent for training as a fighter pilot. In September 1915 he was back in France with Captain's rank, commanding the only formed flight of the new Vickers FB5s in France as part of Brooke-Popham's No. 5 Squadron. Under good instructors he had become a much better pilot and seems to have been little bothered by his myopia. A month later, exactly upon St. Crispin's day, and helped by Eric Lubbock, the son of Lord Avebury, as observer, he shot down a German. The battle did not last long but it demonstrated the improvement that had come about in Robert's skill at handling a machine in the air. Before they were a thousand feet up he spotted two enemy aircraft in the distance coming towards him. There was time enough to get another 8,000 feet of altitude before they met and he was able to tell Lubbock exactly how he intended to deal with them. The leading German, an early mark of

Albatros, came nose to nose at him, whereupon Robert pulled
the Vickers into a steep climb. As the German pilot followed
suit Robert changed course and dived underneath with only
about five feet between the pair of them. Both he and Lubbock
opened up with their Lewis guns and scored a number of hits
before both stopped. The Vickers went into a dive, nearly
throwing Lubbock out of his seat, and it was only when the
ground was within a hundred feet that Robert was able to
straighten it out. By then the German had crashed. Robert
recovered himself, Lubbock cleared the stoppages in both
guns, and they set off eastwards again after the second enemy.
Loraine had exhausted his luck for the day; the Vickers was a
sturdy aircraft but it was not to be tossed and wrenched about
in this fashion. The engine protested and died before contact
was made, leaving Robert with his work cut out to glide back
over our own lines and make a forced landing in a field. It was
not really the kind of victory to brag about, for the German
pilot was no Immelmann nor was his machine as good as the
Vickers, but it was a demonstrable success and both Loraine
and Lubbock were given Military Crosses for it. More likely
the award came to Robert to mark a long term of outstanding
bravery in the air and for his example in helping to make the
RFC tradition of always attacking everything everywhere. At a
time when the Germans had the better machines and weapons
it was not always easy to keep young pilots up to the collar and
the D'Artagnan spirit was badly needed. Robert had got inside
the skin of the part and was happier than he had ever been. In
an account of his first fight he wrote of "the joy of battle" and
"satisfaction over winning a fight" without the smallest feeling
of bombast. This was the way of the Flying Corps. On the next
day his Vickers flew over the German aerodrome merely to
drop a bag containing a letter and some personal gear. "To
O.C. FELDFLIEGE-ABTIELUNG 23. The machine
piloted by Unter-Offizier Gerold was shot down by an English
battle-plane on October 26 in the British lines. Unter-Offizier
Gerold, although mortally wounded, made a gallant but
unsuccessful effort to fly back to his own lines. He died a few

minutes after he was taken out of the machine and is buried
near Ration Farm Le Rossignol, opposite Messines. His grave
is marked with a cross with his name, rank and date. Lieut.
Bucholz was slightly wounded and is a prisoner of war.
Herewith effects of Unter-Offizier Gerold. Please acknowledge
receipt of them as listed on the envelope." Bernard Shaw, who
was constantly writing sniggering letters, could not resist a
rather obvious quotation from *The Ancient Mariner* about shooting Albatrosses.

Within No. 5 Squadron Loraine was cordially disliked. He
was just on 40 and had seen much of life. The average age of the
other pilots was about 19 and they had seen little outside their
college closes. At that date a pilot, his machine and his
mechanic formed something like the mediaeval lance, a self-
contained fighting unit that would work with others while
retaining a large degree of independence. They did not like
being ordered about. It would have been bad enough coming
from a real officer but to be humbugged by a jumped-up
strolling player was not to be endured. Robert was never
tactful with his juniors and certainly tended to treat subalterns
as he had used to treat Vedrines. The day came when the Mess
had enough and resolved to form up in a body to Brooke-
Popham and present a mass request for transfers unless Captain Loraine went. Being well-conducted young men they
agreed that first one delegate should tell the offender what they
were doing. Robert proved surprisingly tractable, promising in
future to stop interfering with other men's machines but
adding that woe betide anyone who was slack. The shade of
Vedrines remained with him and he was for ever fiddling with
engines and gadgets; it had to be admitted that he improved
the performances of both engines and aircraft more than did
any other man. A kind of *modus vivendi* was reached; the young
men all reckoned themselves better pilots and kinder to their
machinery – in which there was much truth – but, as the
delegate said of him, "he has the guts of a lion". Some degree of
forgiveness must have come; the Adjutant was heard to say to a
visiting General, "a marvellous old man, you see, sir. Gets into

his plane without the help of a ladder." They continued to put up with him, wincing as he over-revved his engines and noticing that whilst they held the stick between finger and thumb "Loraine always held it with his fist as a barmaid draws a pint". All the same, he flew daily as a scout pilot, save when the awful cold put his remaining lung almost out of action, until March 1916 when he was sent home to Gosport for a course on the new fighters that were to knock the Fokker out of the sky.

Robert survived the course. Towards the end of August 1916 he was given a step to Major and was back in France, commanding one of the first all-fighter squadrons, the newly-raised No. 40. Its aircraft were FE8s, single-seater pushers with a performance far better than anything he had known before. Trenchard knew what he was doing, for it was not the Major's business to fly except on rare occasions. His was the harder part, waiting on the tarmac at sunrise, the Sergeant-Major his only companion, and slowly counting the number of machines that flew or staggered back to land.

In the bitter winter of early 1917 the future Marshal of the Royal Air Force Lord Douglas happened to be at Treizennes and encountered No. 40 Squadron. "The whole atmosphere was dominated by the character of Robert Loraine and . . . his organization was stage-managed with a masterly touch. A fire broke out in one of the hangars in which there were four of No. 40's aircraft, and it quickly raged through the petrol tanks and the wood and the canvas wings of the aircraft. There was nothing that any of us could do, and we just stood around and watched the blaze. But suddenly, reflected in the light from the fire, there appeared in front of us the arresting figure of Loraine, a presence, and it was as if he had stepped out from the wings to take up his position in front of the foot-lights. This was the occasion for the star to play his part, and play it he did. Unbuttoning his trousers and aiming in the direction of the fire, he performed almost with contempt, and certainly with defiance . . . a perfectly natural function."

In truth, he was playing the lead in *Pagliacci*. His nerves had already been stretched near to breaking and the steady flow of losses amongst his young pilots was affecting him more than he cared to show. The last straw came with the death of George Smart, who had returned to an army in which he had served at Omdurman and had just fallen at the head of his battalion. From that moment Robert became a morose immitigable figure. He drove 40 Squadron relentlessly until it became one of the best in France but neither it nor he took the pride in this that was their due. He began to feel his age and it was plain to see that the happy warrior in him was dead.

Robert kept up the regular Mess "beanos", acting furiously all the time to keep up the spirits of the youngsters, but there was no more joy of battle. In March 1917 he went home for three months, returning in June as a Lieutenant-Colonel in command of 14 Wing, with a DSO added to his other ribbons. The change in him, however, could not be hidden and within a month he was sent home to take over a training establishment.

Loraine hated the training school and it hated him. He seems to have been playing Strindberg rather than Shaw, the Father in place of the Chocolate Soldier, and he treated the young aspirants with near brutality. A footnote in his biography, by C. G. Grey, the doyen of historians of the air, reads, "The RAF could do with a few disciplinarians of his type to-day, now that all sorts of unlicked youngsters are coming into it." It was written in 1938. Robert forced those he reckoned shirkers into the air, over-ruled medical reports that pupils were too ill to fly and was to some extent responsible for the high casualty rate. Nobody could accuse him of hanging back himself; were he to be told that a machine was unserviceable he would take it up himself, arguing that if a pilot as clumsy as he could fly it then anybody could. By the spring of 1918, surrounded by discontent, he announced that he would sooner be shot down a thousand times than supervise the training of unmentionables who did not wish to be schooled. He expressed himself willing to take a drop in rank as the price of getting away and in May 1918, in the black days after the March Retreat, he was back in France commanding a squadron of bombers. His judgment of the young had been no better than

Grey's. It was the most suitable job for him. Air fighting now was a mass-produced business with swarms of sophisticated machines where a few years before only a few museum-pieces had operated. He would have been useless as a fighter pilot now but Robert was not going to be kept out of the sky. With night bombers driving deep over the German lines he would be as good as the next man. For two months, possibly the most critical two months of the war, Major Loraine flew mission after mission, bombing German communications and dumps in preparation for Haig's final advance to victory.

July 1918 saw the deaths of Mannock and McCudden, the men who, with Albert Ball, bore the greatest names in military flying. It also marked the end of the flying career of Robert Loraine. Once again it was fire from the ground that got him, three bullets smashing the joint of his left knee, tearing away the cap and the knuckle-end of both bones. The doctors in France, overworked to dropping, wished to amputate but Robert would not hear of it. Shaw wrote one of his tee-heeing letters about one-legged Hamlets which did little to cheer him. By being a nuisance Robert compelled the Base Hospital to rid itself of him and he was sent to London. There surgeons undertook to try and avoid treatment so drastic, but they were not encouraging. Robert lay on the broad of his back, in great pain and gloomily contemplating the plaster cylinder that had been his leg. He was 42, possessed nothing but a chestful of medals and a problematical pension, and had to make a living in the only way he knew. When he was told that he must stay like this for five months and then, with luck, he would have a leg that would never be other than straight he became desperate; he broke the plaster, and deliberately bent the stump inwards. The hospital authorities washed their hands of him, or threatened to, and it was the Profession that came to the rescue. Irene Vanbrugh, a regular visitor, was a friend to Sir Alfred Fripp and Fripp was to arms and legs what Vedrines had been to struts and spars. He constructed an artificial joint and before the Armistice was signed Robert was walking.

The remainder of his history has nothing to do with flying

but it would be absurd to end the story here. As soon as he had been demobilized he was signed up by Charles B. Cochran to play Cyrano de Bergerac for the next three years at £7,000 a year. The part might have been created with him in mind and no doubt memories of the Vedrines *frères* helped. Within months they split up; Loraine took over the show in its entirety and did very well with it: Cochran complained that it had cost him £8,000. His popularity was greater than ever and he began to cheer up again. There came a series of Shaw plays which ended their friendship when Shaw accused Loraine of taking drugs. J. M. Barrie took his place, inviting Robert to play in *Mary Rose*. He was not enthusiastic; before deciding he went for a flight over the Alps in a hired aeroplane, lost his way, landed in Bavaria and was interned for a week as a spy. Barrie persuaded him to take the part and the play ran for a year. Then, at the end of 1921, he sailed for New York on a kind of sabbatical and made his way to Hollywood. He thought little of the place and continued his cruise round the world, acquiring a new wife in the process. From then on it was plays and more plays, in London and New York. After *Cyrano,* several times revived, his most acclaimed piece of work was as Adolf in Strindberg's *The Father,* a part for which his own sufferings had prepared him. He made a lot of money and he lost a lot of money, the Great Slump helping to empty his treasury. In 1934, in the middle of a furious quarrel with Alexander Korda over the film rights of *Cyrano,* he was taken ill and died suddenly. His *Who's Who* entries show Robert's assessments of the relative values of things. All about the Isle of Wight and Irish Sea flights, the bare bones of his war-time doings and not a word about the stage. He was surely the best judge.

CHAPTER TWO

Robin Hood

Albert Ball

Ask any ten knowledgeable people for the name of the most famous of RFC pilots and the chances are that eight at least will say "Ball". It is not so much that the name is short and easily memorable as the fact that he was the first of a long line and the man whom all his successors took as their model. When he died three months before attaining the legal age of majority there can hardly have been a man in England unfamiliar with his exploits.

Nottingham is about as near as one can get to the heart of England; there Balls have long enjoyed positions of civic importance. The Sheriff of Nottingham has for centuries been an under-appreciated figure in childhood stories and Albert Ball seems to have inherited the qualities of some ancestor more probably to be found in the outlaw camp. He was a marksman of Robin's own class and the society of such as Will Scarlet, Friar Tuck and Alan a'Dale would have been congenial to him, for he never conformed to the type of little grey men who never did anything wrong or anything different.

Albert was born in 1896, the elder son of a highly-respectable Nottingham estate agent and councillor, who also dabbled in engineering. At grammar school and at Trent College his interests were always severely practical, with chemistry and mechanics well ahead of the older forms of learning. He messed about with scrapped engines, with explosives, with wireless and with electric light plants and by the time he was 17 he had acquired an interest, so far as a legal infant could do such a thing, in an engineering firm partly owned by his father. He also discovered himself to be an excellent instinctive pistol shot. By 1914 young Albert seemed set for a distinguished career in some form of the engineering which dominated the English Midlands and on the way to becoming Sheriff of Nottingham himself. Then the storm burst, and Albert Ball, like all the best of the young men, went for a soldier; he joined Nottingham's own regiment, the Sherwood Foresters. His training in the Trent College Cadet Corps made him a valuable acquisition and within a fortnight, at just 18, he was made up to Sergeant. By October 1914 he had received his commission and was bored. The regular Foresters had been in the thick of it, from Mons to the Aisne and then north to Ypres. Their casualties, like those of most good county regiments, had been dreadful but Ball's Territorial battalion was still held back for home defence and his contribution to victory was to balance the canteen accounts. In the hope of getting to France he transferred to a cyclist battalion but, apart from the exercise, the move did nothing to help him.

In the summer of 1915 his battalion was stationed at Luton. Ball, with little to do, was turning an honest penny by buying and selling motor-cycles and thus he was becoming better off than most subalterns. His commercial activities took him fairly often to London and he appears to have marked down with interest the flying activity at Hendon. Being comparatively rich he decided to lay out some of his money in taking flying lessons, rather in the spirit in which another man might have taken up music or fretwork. The Ruffi-Bauman School, which boasted a Caudron aeroplane, agreed to take him on at a fee of £75, an enormous sum for an ordinary subaltern. Ball signed up and paid. Lessons had to be fixed at times that did not clash with his routine duties, in consequence of which he arranged to be given his instruction very early in the morning. There used to be a saying, well known in both flying services though it was of naval origin, that "the worst thing about this somewhat unpleasant war is that many estimable English gentlemen are required to take an active interest in affairs before the world has been properly aired and warmed". Ball no longer cared, for he had discovered a way of life so exhilarating that everything else seemed of small account. Before he got his Royal Aero Club certificate in October 1915 his application for transfer to the RFC was in. The customary interview with Lord Hugh Cecil took place at the War Office and Cecil obviously liked what he saw. He made the usual offer; Ball could go to France as an observer and take his chance of becoming a pilot later on. Albert was having none of that. He had paid a lot of money for his training and would prefer to have it given a polish by the RFC after which he would become a pilot straight away. It sounded good sense to Lord Hugh who had him posted to Norwich.

Several of the greatest pilots were unpromising as fledglings. Bishop never learned to make a decent landing, Lufbery would have been turned out had not everybody liked him so much and Robert Loraine cost the taxpayer a lot of money in his time. None, however, seems to have been quite as bad as Albert Ball. Very probably his civilian training was a disadvantage, for this was still the old army and nobody suffered as much as the cavalry recruit who said that he could ride a horse. It is also possible that the instructors were not of first quality. Young Albert could tell a good man from a second-rater and was never afraid to speak his mind. After he had had several crashes, though none was serious, an exasperated teacher told him that he would never let him fly again. Ball replied that if this were so he had better go back to his cyclists at once, for he had no inclination to hang around watching others. He was given one last chance, to be taken immediately in another of the School's Maurice Farmans. Ball, concentrating very hard, made five perfect landings in a row.

A look at Albert Ball on the eve of his departure for France might not come amiss. He was a well-favoured young man and, like so many pilots, below the average height at about five feet five. (He was a giant compared to Beauchamp-Proctor who, at barely five feet, had to have a cockpit specially built for him.) By nature he was quiet and thoughtful, with excellent manners and sound commercial instincts. No doubt most pilots in the privacy of their own minds had a genuine belief in the Christian faith but few showed any evidence of it. Years of compulsory chapels at school had given them a surfeit of the outward show of religion but Ball was not ashamed to show it. Evensong was his chosen time and he never missed a service if he could help it. A few years ago that wise man Harold Macmillan observed that he dated the decline of England from the time when people ceased to attend church regularly, and Ball would have agreed with him. His other form of relaxation was to learn the violin. Whether he was any good with the instrument cannot be said with certainty, for those who heard him play – always to himself, never at a concert – were not good judges. Wherever he found himself for more than a very short period Albert Ball also insisted on making a garden, however small, and this was a subject he fully understood. He was merry enough, as became his age, but he did not smoke, drank little, and the muliebrity of such places as Charlie's Bar in Amiens had no attraction for him. Early in the war he had become engaged to a girl at home and that was sufficient for him. His own form of unwinding was to light a red magnesium flare outside his hut and walk round it in pyjamas scraping away at his violin. As General Sir Hope Grant had had the same habit during the Indian Mutiny, reading wood-fire for flare, there must be something to commend it.

In January 1916 Ball qualified as an RFC flier and, after a week or two instructing at Gosport, he embarked for France to become a BE2c pilot with No. 13 Squadron. It was not the kind of work for which he was cut out, lumbering over the German lines directing artillery fire and occasionally, as a treat, being allowed to drop a small bomb. His story nearly came to an abrupt end after the first fortnight, when he was attacked over the German trenches by a Fokker. No BE would have had much of a chance at the best of times; the observer's gun jammed after a couple of rounds and Ball tried a shot with his pistol which misfired. By good fortune there had been time enough for them to reach home ground and the Fokker sheered off. A little later on he was shot down by anti-aircraft fire but again his luck was in. The machine crash-landed inside the British lines and both Ball and his observer scrambled out unhurt. All the time he was learning fast and it became plain – certainly to outsiders and possibly to Ball himself – that he was one of those happy men who are incapable of fear. In his waddling BE he attacked machines against which it had as much chance as a portly alderman matched with a professional boxer. Not only did he survive these encounters but he frightened his enemies away and even came within a whisker of the near-miraculous feat of shooting one down. It happened on 3 May, during the long build-up for the Somme. Ball and his observer were caught by five enemy aircraft, every one capable of making a meal of them. He drove straight in and scattered them, whereupon a two-seater Albatros appeared heading straight for him. Ball took him on, in a battle of nerves where one of them must break; his observer killed the German gunner and the Albatros pilot gave Ball best, diving hurriedly away. News that the RFC had come by a flier out of the common run must have been bruited about, for soon after this Albert Ball was selected to become a fighter pilot.

It was the moment of the war when, as Lord Kitchener had prophesied and for which he had planned, France had passed her peak and Britain was getting into her stride. The best of the RFC's aircraft were, however, still French and the machines that would drive the Germans from the sky were in the blue-print or mock-up stage. The Fokker and the Albatros were reckoned better than anything yet available to either Ally and the German end of the eternal see-saw was uppermost. No RFC name equalled those of Immelmann and Boelcke and it was the right time for one to emerge. Ball went to the aircraft depot to see what it had to offer. First, he tried a Morane scout, fitted with an interrupter gear of an early kind which it was hoped would let it meet the Fokker on level terms. A tentative burst of fire blew the propeller to pieces; it needed a good pilot to bring the machine home, but there was nothing lacking in Ball's skill now and he coaxed it down in one piece. Next he tried a Nieuport, at a happy moment when a German appeared over the aerodrome and needed seeing off. The machine seemed promising but at first pressure the Bowden cable operating the gun broke; Ball dashed back, exchanged the Nieuport for a Bristol and took off again. By then the German had gone.

In his new capacity as hired assassin – the words were in common use – Ball joined No. 11 Squadron, at a time when the Germans were having it too much their own way. No. 11 flew BEs, for there were few, if any, fighter squadrons in existence, and it was Ball's business to look after them as far as one man could do it. The task was impossible of success, for the RFC machines were "cold meat" – their own expression – and he found himself in the position of Sir Boyd Roche; "not being a bird, he could not be in two places at the same time". In a single week No. 11 Squadron lost a complete flight; in one day No. 13 lost six machines. Ball began to score, but it made little difference.

His first kill was an Albatros two-seater, twenty miles on the wrong side of the lines. He took it in the conventional hawk's way by stooping at speed from 12,000 feet to 5,000 and tearing the victim to pieces as he dropped on it. The Bristol in which he did this was not to his liking and he exchanged it for a Nieuport Scout, the machine that remained his favourite until the end. It was the most agile aeroplane in service and in Ball it found a master. The state of affairs in the air, frightening though it was, accorded well with his temperament, for he would attack anything anywhere. There was nothing of the grim Ironside about him, for his letters assured his family that it was all enormous fun and he obviously meant it. After some thought he developed a method of fighting never tried before. The Lewis gun on the Nieuport was so mounted that the pilot could, if he wished, pull the handle down as if to change the drum and fire almost straight upwards. To neglect such a gift would be a pity and Ball decided to take advantage of it. In single combat it was all very well to come down on your enemy from above and sweep him away; his friends, however, would then have an excellent chance of doing the same thing to you. How much better, as you would always be fighting at odds of several to one, to practise flying underneath an opponent and using the gun as a tin-opener. Ball, a fine shot, practised. He would never be able to stand off, as McCudden did, drawing a bead through an Aldis telescopic sight, shooting down an enemy from something like a quarter of a mile. His task would always be in-fighting and it was in tactics suited to this that he must excel.

Sholto Douglas sums up Albert Ball's way of fighting by saying that he would "dash madly into the middle of any number of enemy aircraft, shoot down a couple of them, and then, knowing just when to pull out, charge off, more often than not having received quite a peppering himself". It probably looked mad, but it was carefully worked out. Ball, high in the air, watched for enemy formations, picked his man and went for him. Other kills followed, by reason of his superb skill and the ability of the Nieuport to take punishment without its wings being torn off. His first fights brought few victims, but more importantly, they broke up formations that would otherwise have prevented the two-seaters from carrying out their essential work of registering the guns for the opening barrages.

Ball was never gregarious, though others enjoyed his company. He preferred to live as he fought, alone in a small hut made for him a couple of miles from the Mess where he could play his violin and cultivate his garden undisturbed; there was nothing eremitical about it, for he dined regularly in the Mess like anybody else, but this suited him well, since he was under nobody's orders as to when and where he flew; his expeditions took place at all times, for he haunted enemy aerodromes in the dawn, waiting for the chance to knock one or two down while they were still yawning, and he hung around again during the evening hour called in France "between the dog and the wolf" awaiting their return. Had he been obliged to lead an ordinary communal life he would have gone very short on sleep. Left to himself, he took his rest as he pleased, though it cannot have amounted to much. In leisure moments the old commercial instincts surfaced; he sold off building plots to his friends for their postwar homes and advised his father to watch for an increase in the price of copper.

His first decoration, the Military Cross, came from a different kind of exploit. Had nobody ever invented the aeroplane, balloons would have remained a very satisfactory way of keeping an eye in the sky. Both sides persevered with them, for they produced valuable results, and both sides expended much ingenuity in protecting them. The "spoof" balloon with a basket full of explosive was only one of their artifices. In mid-June, with only days to go before the battle was due to open, a great effort was made to knock down all the Germans in one blow. Ball was caught up in it, as were most fighter pilots. He missed his target at the first attempt, went home to re-arm, and tried again. Every balloon was the centre of a cone of the heaviest anti-aircraft fire of all kinds; Ball, with his usual coolness, flew slowly over the allotted gas-bag, dropped his little bombs and waited for it to ignite. As soon as he saw it to be burning nicely, he went home, hotly pursued by missiles of all kinds. The German gunners got their revenge next day, blowing a cylinder off his engine as he was satisfying his curiosity about an unusual number of transport vehicles. The Nieuport had a good gliding angle and he came home safely without an engine but with enough information to turn the artillery on to a rewarding target.

On 1 July 1916, the worst day in the history of the British Army, Ball was overhead intent on business. Though he could plainly see the long smoking lines of the shell-bursts, with hordes of khaki figures moving behind them and dropping in their hundreds, the day was for him uneventful. The next one made up for it. Two Albatrosses sought him out, one driving straight at him, the other waiting its opportunity. Ball, once more, kept his nerve longer than did his adversary and quickly disposed of the first; then he turned on the second and within five minutes it was crashing to join its companion. With six

aircraft and a balloon notched up Albert Ball was plainly a
coming man. General Trenchard, who badly needed such
encouragement, came in person to congratulate him. For the
next fortnight Ball was hardly ever out of the air but the German
superiority still continued. The strain was more than any man
could bear and Ball, always a practical man, asked if he might
not have a few day's rest. He was given it, in a sense, by being
put back to flying BEs. It was probably not as brutal as it
sounds, for had Ball been grounded even for a time it might have
broken his nerve, since the worst strain always comes after the
battle is over. For a month he went back to artillery-spotting and
some bombing in formation. In mid-August he returned to his
old trade of solitary hunter, long enough to shoot down three out
of a group of twelve and to be brought down for want of petrol
after a running fight with fifteen far over the German lines. He
just managed to make a safe landing in friendly territory. Then
came a change of RFC policy with the creation of proper fighter
squadrons. Ball was posted to one of the best of them, Jack
Scott's No. 60, as a Flight Commander. He had mixed feelings
about it, for he had enjoyed his Robin Hood kind of outlaw
existence; against that, there was something to be said for
having friends watching your tail.

The re-organization was overdue, for the RFC was taking
casualties at a rate that would soon become unendurable. The
battle of the Somme cost more than 300 pilots and just over 200
observers dead, wounded or missing; the fun had gone out of
air-fighting and it was now a grim business. Ball took it in his
stride. As Captain he was punctilious, encouraging the
younger men – at 20, he had still younger men under his
command – and setting an example of almost insane daring
that every new boy tried to imitate. He was, like all the great
fighters, meticulous in his care of the engine and the gun upon
which everything depended; early on he decided that he fought
better flying with neither helmet nor goggles, preferring the feel
of the wind combing violently through his black hair to the
constriction of tight-fitting leather. In this he had few follow-
ers, but the regular Lewis gun practice upon which he insisted

paid a good dividend. It is not always easy to hit a stationary target with a light automatic even when lying comfortably on a groundsheet; to hit an aeroplane flying at 100 mph is difficult; to hit the same aeroplane from another travelling at much the same velocity ought to be impossible except by the purest chance, but experience showed that it could be, and was, done. Like the violin, however, skill demanded unremitting practice.

His new responsibilities did not prevent Ball from keeping up his displays of virtuosity. As soon as the Flight had landed after carrying out its regular patrol he would take himself off to his hut and after a spell of rest he would be in the air again alone. His Nieuport Scout became known to all fliers of both sides from the colour of the spinner fixed to the propeller boss; he had it painted scarlet and at the sight of this a wise German made himself scarce. His score mounted steadily, like that of a batsman who had played himself in, and within a week of joining No. 60 it had doubled from six to twelve, not counting several doubtfuls and the balloon. On the last day of August he charged single-handed into a dozen Germans, sabred down a couple of them and returned without a scratch. A DSO joined his MC but the honours, unheard of for a boy of undergraduate age, never went to his head. Albert Ball remained always the same, quiet, courteous and helpful, never criticizing harshly but always ready with practical advice. Though nobody's boon companion he was liked by all who knew him, even by the hearties whose private relaxations were of a less circumscribed kind. Differing from most of his brother officers he had little respect for the German pilots, describing them as sad fellows without much guts but trying to do their best. It may be, of course, that he was whistling in a graveyard for the good of his juniors but the contemptuous way in which he would take on any number suggests that it was his true opinion.

Good though Ball was, he did not always have things his own way, for there came a moment when he met a man as good as himself. Nobody ever found out the name of the German, but he was a fine pilot. He and Ball chanced to meet alone and Ball, inevitably, lowered his head and charged; this time he had met an enemy who did not flinch and it took some very quick thinking to avoid a head-on ramming that would have finished both of them. Then followed the prettiest tournament ever seen; the machines were equally matched, each pilot was a master and each tried every trick in his repertoire. They turned and swooped, dived and spun, fired away lots of ammunition but did no damage to each other; both appeared to be enjoying it and neither seemed to give a thought to what his end might be. The victory must lie with the man whose nerve cracked and tried to get away, for then his adversary would be on his tail and the show would be over. Thus it went on, the firing becoming slacker and slacker until both realized that they had exhausted their ammunition. After that there was only one thing to be done; Englishman and German flew side by side, roaring with laughter and waving to each other; then they went home. Ball was as delighted as Robin had been at his chance-encounter with Will Scarlett.

When the Somme battle had petered out and Ball's score stood at thirty-two Scott decided that his champion needed a proper rest. He was now a very considerable figure, his DSO was augmented by two bars and a Russian Order had been added to the tally. His score far exceeded anything yet chalked up to any flier on either side and he had an inevitable propaganda value. Mr. Lloyd George demanded to meet him; Nottingham made him the only freeman known to be so honoured whilst a legal infant and he was sought by everybody who was anybody. Albert, mildly amused by it all, had no appetite for staying in England so long as there was work to be done in France. His fiancée made no attempt to dissuade him, though she must have seen the likelihood of becoming a widow before she was a wife. Nottingham used to boast – perhaps it does still – of turning out the most beautiful girls in England; one sample suggests that they need fear no competition in other qualities.

Ball served a turn at instructing but his heart was never in it. The smell of cordite and castor oil worked on him like blood on a war-horse and when he heard that a new Squadron, No. 56, was forming and was to be equipped with the latest thing in

fighting aircraft he pulled the necessary wires to get himself
into it. Major Blomfield was determined that No. 56, though
all its traditions were in front of it, was going to be something
more than just another numbered unit. When he learnt that
Captain Ball was at large he snapped him up. Ball was more
than willing to be snapped and he inspected the SE5 narrowly.
The little chocolate-coloured biplane inspired confidence at
first glance, though Ball quickly spotted its weak points. It was
good to look at, a fair indication of its likely performance, and
the stationary Hispano-Suiza engine was more powerful than
anything of its kind so far. Its armament was impressive; a
Vickers gun, no longer using the infantry canvas belt that
waved in the breeze when empty but an affair of disintegrating
links copied from an Austrian design, fired through the propeller under the control of an ingenious system worked by oil-
pressure, and made it possible to fire much longer bursts than
the Lewis with its drum of only forty-seven rounds. (The
ninety-four-round drum existed but was not yet in common
use). The SE promised speed in level flight and whilst diving, it
would zoom upwards almost on its tail, but one aspect of it
troubled Ball slightly. The weight was all in the front and it did
not seem likely that it would turn as quickly as the rotary-
engined Nieuport. Experiment soon showed him to be right. Its
fire-power – it had a Lewis gun mounted above the top wing in
addition to the Vickers – and its turn of speed made it ideal in
formation work but the Nieuport was the polo pony compared
with the hunter. Ball adopted the sensible plan of "horses for
courses", and struck a bargain. He would gladly join 56 as a
Flight Commander of SEs but he wanted a Nieuport Scout of his
own for the private expeditions which he had no intention of
abandoning. This presented no difficulty.

On 7 April 1917 Ball arrived with his Squadron over the big
aerodrome of Vert Galand, alongside the road from Doullens
to Amiens. The German pilots were still in the ascendancy,
their best man being Oswald Boelcke with a score in the high
thirties, and the RFC was taking terrible pounding. During
that month, the month of the Arras battle in which Vimy Ridge

was the Allies' objective, about 140 machines had been shot down, ninety of them being artillery-spotting two-seaters of obsolete pattern. Ball felt that there was no time to waste; leaving his Flight to land at Vert Galand and sort itself out, he set off towards the German lines and shot down number thirty-three.

The old tactics were still working. Once again Ball had his private establishment set up, his equivalent of the clearing in Sherwood Forest, and he did not spare himself. On top of the ordinary duties of a Flight Commander, quite enough in themselves for most men, he used his private armoury of two SEs and a Nieuport with a roving commission to act as he thought best. On the evening of 26 April, having already added ten to the game-book, he set about a formation of five Albatrosses and sent two of them spinning down in his old style. The Vickers was – still is – a splendid gun, but it has a thirst for ammunition. Ball, run dry, had to lose himself in the clouds avoiding the pursuing survivors until it was dark enough to make a dash for home. By early May he was shooting down enemy aeroplanes at the rate of two a day and his name was in everybody's mouth. For this there was a price, and even Ball's nerves were not exempt from strain. At the end of his first week there came a battle between his SE and two well-handled Albatrosses; he cut down the first and turned to meet the second head-on in his usual style. The brave German stared him out and although Ball riddled him with the Vickers he managed before going down to get in a burst from his Spandau that badly damaged Ball's engine. When he got back to Vert Galand Ball was so badly shocked that it was a long time before he could give a coherent account of what had happened. The candle was beginning to gutter, but Ball would not hear of rest until the battle was won and the RFC on top once more.

Almost more upsetting to him was the loss of his private camp. In the course of a concert given by the Squadron's orchestra – one of Blomfield's pleasant conceits – word came in that it was on fire. By the time Ball arrived all was gutted, hut, bathroom and greenhouse. From then onwards he had to make do with a tent. The zest was going out of everything, as his letters to his fiancée and his father show. "Am indeed looked after by God, but oh! I do get tired of always living to kill, and am really beginning to feel like a murderer." "I hate this game, but it is the only thing one must do just now." He never let up. Evening, as for owls and bats, was the best killing-time and the sound of Ball's engine coming home in the dusk was a regular part of 56 Squadron's daily life. Even after his encounter with two Albatrosses he had been up again within a couple of hours, flying his Nieuport and knocking down a straggler.

On the evening of 7 May eleven SEs of No. 56 Squadron, Ball's amongst them, set out in poor visibility trailing their coats in front of the Germans. The clouds thickened and the formation split up. Four red Albatrosses swooped down on them and in an instant all eleven were fighting for their lives. Six machines were lost that night, five of them being accounted for, but Ball was never seen again. The last glimpse of his machine was caught by Cecil Lewis, as it flew straight into a great white cloud. The pilots of No. 56, scarcely believing that they would never again hear the engine bringing Ball home through the long shadows of a summer night, dropped a message over Douai asking for news. Later it was learned that he had been buried with all honour at Annoeuillin, a dozen miles east of La Bassee. Even his enemies did not know the exact circumstances of his death, for it took three weeks for them to answer. First it was thought that he had fallen to Lothar von Richtofen but later it was ascertained that his machine had almost certainly been hit by anti-aircraft fire.

His Victoria Cross was posthumous, his end, like Robin's, uncertain. The RFC never saw his like again. Soon many men were to pass his score of forty-four but no one of them had to fight as Albert Ball had fought, one against many and over and over again. Is it wonderful that eight men out of ten, asked to name the greatest of the RFC's many great fighters, will almost certainly answer "Ball"?

CHAPTER THREE

The Regular

J. T. B. McCudden

Captain Bertram Dickson of the Royal Field Artillery was the first British officer to fly. In 1910 he left the Army to join what was to become the Bristol Aeroplane Company and when in the following year he was asked his opinion about recruiting for the Air Battalion RE he gave an interesting answer. "One man is a rich man; another man is an artist or he is an actor; another man is a mechanic. They are funny fellows. You will get a certain number if you pay them well, because they are out for making money; you will get others who will do it for sport, and others who will do it for the advertisement." In this there was much truth, but none of the caps fitted the boy who became one of the greatest fighter pilots of them all.

James Thomas Byford McCudden joined the Royal Engineers in 1910 as a boy-bugler of 15 because the McCuddens were an Army family and the Sappers were the family corps. His father was a warrant officer, his brother Bill had signed on four years earlier and another of the four boys would follow him later. Bill was a founder-member of the Royal Flying Corps, to which he was transferred in May 1912 from the old Balloon Section. He had taken his Royal Aero Club aeroplane pilot's certificate on joining – a rare thing for a man below commissioned rank – and qualified for his RFC wings two months later. Jimmy first put on the fencer's jacket of the Corps in April 1913, well pleased with what he thought "would suit my rather erratic temperament".

The Sappers have always drawn their recruits from more promising young men than those given to the infantry of the line, but the McCuddens were still a cut above the average. There was French blood in them, along with blood of both northern and southern Ireland, and they were poles apart from the ordinary run of beer-swilling squaddies who thronged the streets of Aldershot. There survives a photograph of the young Jimmy, taken soon after his arrival at Farnborough. The pleasant, manly face, the perfectly kept uniform, polished boots and immaculately rolled puttees show a miniature of that magnificent army that sent the BEF to Mons, Le Cateau and to Ypres. It is not a type of face often seen now, at any rate amongst civilians.

Such mechanical knowledge as he possessed on reaching Blenheim Barracks had been gained from his motor-cycle – which never went except by pedalling – but it was still more than most men had. The RFC, according to him, owned twenty-three assorted aircraft; a fly-past would have enchanted a lepidopterist but disheartened a budding aviator. On the strength of owning a motor-cycle, still reposing at Farnborough station – he had paid £3 for it and eventually gave it to the station-master in lieu of storage charges – he was posted to the Flying Depot and given charge of a 70 hp Renault engine, the motive power of a Maurice Farman. His first task was to perfect himself at propeller-swinging on an inoffensive-looking little Caudron. This kept him occupied during the morning; in the afternoon he was promoted to rubbing rust off the wires of the Maurice Farman. Having finished this by tea-time and with nothing more to do, McCudden wandered over to the Caudron and gave the propeller a tentative swing. It appeared that somebody else had been killing time with it, "wondering what the difference was between the little tap on the right and the little lever on the left, etc.", and had abandoned the machine, leaving the switch on and throttle wide open. McCudden's tug was answered by a roar and the Caudron leapt at him, just missing him with its lower wing as he dropped flat, and attacked the Maurice Farman standing in the doorway. By the time it had destroyed two tail-booms and half a wing McCudden managed to get inside and switch the thing off. The hangar was thick with castor oil smoke, mechanics appeared squirting fire extinguishers in all directions and, after a heavy silence, the voice of Major Raleigh was heard. "Sergeant-Major! Fall in two men." Off to the guard-room went 2nd. Class Air Mechanic McCudden, J. During the few days when he was under open arrest awaiting trial he encountered Lieut. B. T. James, the RFC's wireless expert, and asked whether he might have a flight with him. James obviously liked his keenness – mechanics hardly ever flew, nor did many of them want to – and gave him a short trip in his BE2a. Jimmy McCudden landed, having greatly enjoyed himself but with the proviso that flying was not so easy as was generally imagined, just in time for CO's Orders. An unfeeling Colonel gave him 168 hours' detention and the glasshouse opened its doors to him.

This may sound like injustice, but it was only to be expected. The Corps' first Adjutant, Basil Barrington-Kennett of the Grenadiers, had sworn a great oath that the RFC should combine the smartness of the Guards with the technical skill of the Royal Engineers. There was no laxity of discipline in the Corps even if it did live in greasy overalls for most of the time.

On returning to circulation, McCudden found himself posted to No. 3 Squadron on Salisbury Plain, under command of Major Brooke-Popham. He was supremely happy. His fellow-mechanics were as congenial company as a man could want, he was on excellent terms with his officers, he had – despite the forfeiture of fourteen days' pay – a new motor-cycle and he was learning all there was to know about engines; rotary engines, radial engines, stationary in-line and Vee engines. Above all, he was getting quite a lot of flying, even if only as a passenger. His particular charge now was a 50 hp Bleriot, a gift to the RFC (another was a present from the Duke of Westminster) from the International Correspondence School. Private charity equipped a substantial part of the Corps. "What a splendid squadron No. 3 was. We had a magnificent set of officers and the NCOs and men were as one family".

In the summer of 1914 McCudden badly wanted to fly but it was not official policy to encourage air mechanics to get ideas above their station. His elder brother, now a Sergeant and one of the few non-commissioned pilots, did what he could for him in the way of instruction but the prospect of ever sitting in a cockpit at the controls of his own aircraft seemed remote. When he arrived in France on 12 August 1914 it was by steamer to Le Havre and not with the flying element of the squadron. McCudden, at 19 and burning with enthusiasm, had to watch the amateur fliers with Special Reserve commissions doing as best they could the job for which he hankered and was so well fitted. "Other ranks" were not yet needed as pilots.

People of an egalitarian turn of mind see in this a disagreeable exhibition of class distinction and this is, up to a point, true. When McCudden was first given command of a squadron there were officers who asked for transfer rather than serve under one who was not a gentleman. It had nothing to do with any dislike of the man, nor were all the people concerned stupid snobs. The matter went deeper. For generations before 1914 there had been, for the Army, only two classes. A man might move up from one to another but rarely (General Sir William Robertson was such a rarity) did he get far. It was instinct, and a very old one. Nor did it mean that the officers hogged the best of everything; the reverse was equally true. Did a grenade fail to explode on a range, it was the officer and nobody else who must risk his skin and destroy it; none but an officer might handle public money, not because the Colour Sergeant could not be trusted but because, if any disappeared, it must be the officer who was held accountable. Piloting an aircraft, being a very dangerous business, was officers' work. After a year of war all this had become history but it does explain how

McCudden and others like him got off to a late start. It would have been quite needless to lecture him in this fashion; everybody in 1914 knew it.

He was happy enough to be in an observer's seat in time to follow the retreat from Mons and to look down on the stand of Smith-Dorrien's II Corps at Le Cateau. His pilot on that occasion was Captain Philip Joubert de la Ferté, quarter of a century later to be AOC Coastal Command. Joubert and L. E. O. Charlton were generally held to be the men who spotted Von Kluck's change of direction and thus brought about the battle of the Marne.

In the summer of 1918 McCudden, then a Major and one of the biggest names in the Flying Corps, wrote his own account of all he had seen and done, giving it to C. G. Grey for editing. It is interesting to notice his complete lack of "side"; the junior officers of whom he speaks when telling of the early days are always respectfully called "Mr", and his own eminence sat lightly upon him. Not a word in the whole book, written in longhand at a speed which Grey reckoned at a thousand words an hour, suggests any self-satisfaction. It is the most modest account imaginable and could only have been written by a man of rare quality.

The retreat, the counter-stroke at the Marne and the attack by the BEF across the Aisne all saw Air Mechanic McCudden working flat out, by day, observing the dropping of makeshift petrol bombs and the useless steel darts called flechettes, and regularly working through the night grinding the valves from Joubert's Gnome in order to get a few more revolutions to the minute out of it. Joubert went home in September and McCudden was taken over by Lieutenant Conran who possessed a two-seater 80 hp Bleriot. He was made up to Corporal in November but life went on in much the same way: observing, driving around the white French roads in a Crossley tender looking for aircraft that had landed in unsought places, repairing their engines and hurrying back for more. It was cold, wet, windy winter and a new experience was added. Large canvas hangars had arrived, neatly erected with deep drainage ditches on three sides. The gales tore them down over the sheltering aircraft and mechanics; splashes and oaths heard faintly above thundering canvas-noises like a windjammer going about in a storm indicated that some had failed to find the way out. At Gonneham aerodrome near St. Omer it took 12 tons of cinders every day to keep a surface from which a machine might take off.

In April 1915 McCudden was promoted Sergeant but his pleasure at reaching full NCO rank was soon eclipsed. In the following month his brother Bill was killed at Gosport whilst instructing a pupil. "This was a bad blow for me as I had always looked up to him so much, and I felt his loss very keenly indeed. However, I suppose it had to be." At the end of June Jimmy was recommended for flying training, but he was not released from his squadron, "as I could not be spared away from my flight because of the engine work". The Fokker monoplane in service a few months later gave Germany a weapon far superior to anything in the British armoury. Boelcke and Immelmann rode almost unchallengeable, chargers pitted against carthorses, and Albert Ball was still a subaltern of foot. McCudden continued his usual work throughout the battle of Loos and watched Immelmann from the ground. His only original contribution to the war was a mousetrap of a complicated kind which cast its victim into a drum of water.

His first air fight came a few days before Christmas 1915. No longer could the Morane Parasols go about their business alone and No. 3 Squadron began to experiment with formation flying designed to give an all-round defence. Bay Harvey-Kelly led the flight of three, the other two following in echelon with Sergeant McCudden clutching an unmounted Lewis gun in the last machine. In a fine cold morning with no wind the little formation worked up to 7,500 feet over Bethune and headed eastward over the German lines. Hard by Douai, McCudden's pilot, Saunders, pointed his hand towards his left front at a long dark brown form "fairly streaking across the sky". "When it got above and behind our middle machine it dived on to it for all the world like a huge hawk on a hapless sparrow." The comparison was exact, for the Fokker's interrupter gear gave it the means of firing dead ahead with its Spandau while the slow Moranes had only the observer's guns with which to seize any fleeting chance of hitting back. "I saw the black crosses on the Fokker's wings, for a Fokker it was, and as it got to close range, Mr. Mealing, the pilot of this middle machine, turned, and thus saved himself, although the Fokker had already hit the machine. The Fokker had by now turned and was coming towards our machine, nose on, slightly above. Not having a gun mounting to fire in that direction, I stood up, with my Lewis gun to the shoulder, and fired as he passed over our right wing. He carried on flying in the opposite direction until he was lost to view. We were by now over Douai aerodrome and, looking down, I could see several enemy machines leaving the ground. I watched them for a while and then noticed the Fokker climbing up under our tail. I told my pilot to turn and then fired half a drum of Lewis at the Fokker at 300 yards range. The Fokker seemed rather surprised that we had seen him and immediately turned off to my left rear as I was facing the tail. After this he climbed about 300 feet above us, and then put his nose down to fire. Having been waiting for him, I opened fire at once, and he promptly pulled out of his dive and retired to a distance of 500 yards, at which distance he remained, for every time he came closer I fired a short burst, which had the desired effect of keeping him at a distance. But now we had reached Valenciennes and were circling round obtaining the desired information which consisted in finding out how much rolling-stock was in Valenciennes station. This was important, for at this time our Intelligence had lost track of a Germany army and was trying to locate it. We got the necessary information and then turned west. While we had been circling over Valenciennes, the Fokker had remained at a respectable distance and was doing vertical turns and such tricks. As soon as we left he followed us, just like a vulture, no doubt waiting for one of us to fall out with engine trouble. By now we were approaching Douai on our homeward journey, and the Fokker went down into Douai aerodrome, as he had no doubt finished his petrol. Over the aerodome we could see numerous specks, just under our level of 8,000 feet, and as we approached we saw they were two-seaters, no doubt those which we saw leaving the ground on our outward journey. However, they had not quite been able to reach our height, and as we flew over them I gave two of them a drum each of Lewis for a present, but I am sorry to say I had no luck. We were now nearing the trenches and 'Archie' too, and we went through a very hot five minutes. A large piece of shell went through the centre section plane just above the pilot's head with a frightful crash. However, we soon crossed the lines and glided down and agreed that life was worth living after all, and landed at 11.50 a.m. Our machine, on inspection, had over thirty shrapnel holes in it."

The engagement shows up an essential difference between the two air services. The RFC, though outmatched, never for a moment gave up its offensive policy and took grievous casualties in keeping up air fighting over the German positions; the Fokker pilot – McCudden was certain of it being Immelmann – was more interested in scalps than unspectacular service. No British pilot would have amused himself with vertical turns while an enemy carried out unmolested an important piece of reconnaissance work. Fine pilot though he was, Max Immelmann (if it was he) seems to have lacked the last ounce.

McCudden and he met once more that same afternoon. At 2.30 Major Ludlow-Hewitt took Jimmy up again, this time to sketch a new trench-line near La Bassee. The Fokker jumped them, this time from a cloud-bank, and once again McCudden put the Lewis gun to his shoulder. Ludlow-Hewitt was an experienced hand; with McCudden firing drum after drum behind him he threw the Morane about until the Fokker became disheartened and made off. "I distinctly noticed that the pilot sat very high in his machine and was wearing the black flying-kit." This was Immelmann right enough. Ludlow-Hewitt was always the favourite pilot during his observing days, and it was these fights of 1915 and early 1916 that formed McCudden's tactical thinking which he carried on unaltered until the end. Exhibitionism was not war. Flights, all flights with serious business to do, must be made in formation, every aircraft, pilot and gunner interdependent on the rest. In this way only would the Flying Corps properly serve the Army of which it formed a part.

On 24 January 1916 McCudden's long-cherished ambition came much nearer, with a posting back to Farnborough for training as a pilot. It seems to have been almost superfluous. With many hours in the air logged away and a greater understanding of engines than most of the instructors possessed, he needed no spoon-feeding. He would probably have qualified in record time had not another of the aspirants crashed the school's only Maurice Farman after Jimmy had had only one hour with it. He hung about Farnborough throughout a vile February and March, getting in only two hours more on an Avro 504 of the type which was becoming the standard trainer. Then he was passed to Gosport where on 16 April he gained his Royal Aero Club certificate and in a matter of days was sent on to the Central Flying School at Upavon to become a scout pilot, the job reserved for the pick of the crop. McCudden was a natural flier and seemed to be without nerves. On his first flight over Salisbury Plain, in a DH1, a machine quite unfamiliar to him and burdened with a passenger, he found himself for the first time spinning into the ground. Most men would have felt their bowels turn to water and would not have been ashamed to admit it. McCudden experienced no more than a mild curiosity and recovered himself almost by instinct. For two months he was kept on as an instructor, logging more than a hundred hours of flying time before he arrived at the pilots' pool in St. Omer to await posting to a squadron. No. 20, at Clairmarais, flew FE2ds with the big Rolls-Royce 250 hp engine; McCudden, most of whose experience was still on "pushers", was well content. The squadron's parish was over the Ypres salient, relatively quiet, while the Somme fighting dragged on away to the south.

McCudden had less than a month with No. 20, for in the early days of August he was moved a few miles to Abeele where his old friend Conran was in command of No. 29, flying the new single-seater DH2, one of the machines intended to be a match for the Fokker. Being the man he was, McCudden went meticulously over every part of his No. 5985 with his mechanic and rigger. The gun he made his own particular charge and there was a pond near Clairmarais conveniently placed for target practice. On this he zeroed whenever time allowed, for the Lewis was to the scout pilot what the ·44 had been to the likes of Buffalo Bill.

On 6 September 1916 he was flying alone at the considerable height of 14,000 feet between Armentieres and Ypres, feeling very cold. The sight of a German two-seater painted white all over and plainly bent on mischief restored his circulation and he set off in pursuit with both of them headed to the east. The DH2 and the German were well matched for speed and, after closing to about a quarter of a mile, McCudden could get no nearer. Both of them, at such a height, could afford to lose a little and their noses pointed down. McCudden, knowing his own ability as a marksman let go a drum of forty-seven rounds, changed it for a full one and fired that also. The German continued on his downward course without making any sort of fight of it. At 2,000 feet he disappeared into a cloud-bank and McCudden went home in disgust. Three days later a report came in of a white two-seater having crashed on the Menin Road and McCudden's score had opened. "This was a very easy German to get for one's first and it bucked me up a lot." The days of big killings were yet to come, on both sides, and it was still out of the common for a pilot to have even one unshared victory.

The comparative restfulness over the Salient continued through the late summer and autumn. It was the time when, by a combination of better fliers and better weapons, the RFC enjoyed an undoubted mastery. On the Somme Albert Ball, a year younger than McCudden, was making a name for himself as the great exponent of the Nieuport XXIII. On 2 July 1916, to the delight of any infantrymen who might have been able to watch, he had shot down two Albatrosses in quick succession, a man gets a right and left of pheasants. He and McCudden flew together in the great dog-fight of 9 November, soon after 29 Squadron had moved down to an aerodrome near Arras. McCudden describes how six aircraft took off at a little before dawn to make a sweep between Albert and Bapaume and how they became reduced by engine trouble to only three, Noakes, Ball and himself. As they flew north from Bapaume six specks appeared in the sky to the east; Germany's latest and best, Albatros DI chasers. The battle that followed was a classic of its kind.

"By now we were fairly in the middle of six of them and were getting a fairly bad time of it, for we were a long way east of the line, so we all knew we had to fight hard or go down. At one time I saw a fat Hun about ten yards behind Ball absolutely filling him with lead, as Ball was flying straight, apparently changing a drum of ammunition, and had not seen that Hun. I could not at the time go to Ball's assistance as I had two Huns after me fairly screaming for my blood. However, Ball did not go down. Noakes was having a good time too, and was putting up a wonderful show. The Huns were co-operating very well. Their main tactic seemed to be for one of them to dive at one of us from the front and then turn away, inviting us to follow. I followed three times, but the third time I heard a terrific clack, bang, crash, rip behind me and found a Hun firing from about ten yards in the rear, and his guns seemed to be firing in my very ears. I at once did a half-roll, and as the Hun passed over me I saw the black and white streamers on his interplane struts. This fellow was the Hun leader, and I had previously noticed that he manoeuvred very well. By now, however, we had fought our way back to our own lines, and all three of us had kept together, which was undoubtedly our salvation, but I had used all my ammunition and had to chase round after Huns without firing at them. However, the Huns had apparently had enough too, and as soon as we got back to our lines they withdrew east. I now had time to look over my machine on my way back to the aerodrome and saw that it was in a bad way. My tail plane was a mass of torn fabric, and various wires were hanging, having been cut by bullets . . . I really think that fight was one of the best I have ever had, although we were outnumbered and the Huns had better machines than we. I had a good look round my machine and found that the Huns had scored twenty-four hits. This was the greatest number I have ever had. I do not believe in being shot about. It is bad or careless flying to allow oneself to be shot about when one ought usually to be able to prevent it by properly timed man-oeuvres." Thus spoke the serious professional. He came near to spoiling his dictum that same afternoon. Over Gommecourt in a moment of euphoria he started to loop his DH2, changed his mind and shot all his Lewis gun drums over the top plane into the "pusher" engine; they smashed the propeller and he was lucky to get out of the wreckage alive.

McCudden, as a pilot, had arrived at about slack water high; the short ascendancy enjoyed by the RFC during the Somme battles was disappearing as new machines like the Albatros and Halberstadt with their 220 hp geared Mercedes engines came into service. Equally important was the German possession of the only decent interrupter gear that would allow a belt-fed machine-gun to fire through the arc of a propeller. M. Constantinescu had long been treated by officials at the War Office as a mad Rumanian professor but by the summer of 1916, after a series of flukes, his invention was being taken up and the Vickers gun with its great capacity for sustained fire would soon be coming to supplement the Lewis. McCudden was still getting his share of inconclusive air-fighting and enjoying it – "but it was no fun fighting an enemy who was 15 miles faster and had almost twice the climb". On 1 January 1917 he went home, to be at last commissioned.

It is interesting to compare photographs of Sergeant McCudden and Second Lieutenant McCudden, taken only weeks apart. The former shows the "knut" hairstyle – central parting, wings swept back – affected by the bright young working man and the well-pressed and polished look of the good Regular NCO; a little later his hair is parted on one side in the usual way, not too carefully brushed, and his uniform appears to have been slept in. He went back to his old Squadron, under Major Grattan-Bellew whom he much liked, and settled down to flying his cold little DH2 in one of the most frigid winters of the century. The cold made little difference, for dog-fights over and around Arras – the part of the Western Front coming into prominence now that the Somme battles were finished – took place on most days. On 23 January, having taken off through snow, McCudden was in the thick of it. "A batch of Hun scouts dropped on to us and we had to fight for it, for we were some way east of the trenches. During the ensuing fight I fired at an Albatros Scout who went down in a dive, but I could not pay much attention to it as I was now attacked by a Hun Scout with a rotary engine and a very close gap which I think may have been a Fokker biplane. He passed across my front slightly above, and so I raised my gun on its mounting and fired at him. At once there was a sudden vibration and a noise, so I stopped my engine and made for the lines with the Hun after me. I could not dive steeply because the engine increased its speed, and also the vibration, as the propeller was broken by some empty cartridge cases falling into it after I had fired at the Hun with my gun raised." One cannot think of everything. He landed safely in a field, and there was no more flying for the next few days. "Directly they put hot water into their radiators and started their engines, the water froze solid." When he did get aloft McCudden swore that it was warmer at 10,000 feet than on the ground.

"The weather still continued very clear, cold and frosty, and every day I was up, waiting about over our lines for Hun two-seaters to come across after I had finished my daily patrol." It was quite usual at this stage of the war for squadrons which happened to possess one or two high-class pilots to allow them to police the air with voluntary patrols on their own. In this way Ball had already made a name and McCudden was coming up close behind. The Military Medal had come his way during his last days as a sergeant-pilot, the Military Cross had joined it during his first month as an officer and it was clear that here was a pilot of unusual quality. The

DH2 did not lend itself to fancy flying and it was by a meticulous care for detail that McCudden was showing results. His victories during February were three in number, all professional jobs carried out with a formation. "If patience and perseverance would meet their just reward I certainly would have got many more Huns than I did, for I was up at every opportunity studying the two-seater's habits, his characteristics, and his different types of machine and methods of working. In fact, this branch of work alone, just studying the habits, work and psychology of the enemy aeroplane crews, constitutes a complete education of great interest."

At the end of February 1917 McCudden went home on leave and at the RFC Club in Bruton Street in London he met Ball. "I must say that I was much impressed by this keen-eyed pilot with his determined jaw . . By Jove, I thought, that man is wonderful. And what an example he has set." McCudden himself was now regarded as an example of what a young pilot should aspire to be and he was sent on a lecture tour of training establishments. At Orfordness he first flew a machine of the coming pattern, a Le Rhone-engined Bristol tractor, and "liked it so much that I plucked up courage enough to do six loops on it on my first flight". From mid-March to mid-April he was an instructor at Joyce Green near Dartford, one of the new airfields set up for the defence of London against Zeppelins. His greatest achievement there was regularly to exorcise the fears of younger men by spinning the DH2 and recovering it, a feat that was usually thought impossible; the "pusher" was now on its way out and was considered a death-trap. McCudden, who had a soft spot for it, insisted that in its day it was one of the best machines in the Corps. One of his pupils was named Mannock, "a typical example of the impetuous young Irishman, and I always thought he was of the type to do or die". Mannock, most unluckily, did both but he maintained that McCudden had at least lengthened his life by demonstrating his spin technique, "which I think at the time was to put all controls central and offer up a very short and quick prayer".

In April he was moved to Dover, still instructing and gaining experience of the new generation of aircraft that were coming out of the factories, mostly the new Vickers models from their experimental establishment which was also at Joyce Green. There, too, he came upon his young brother Anthony, 19 years old and undergoing his elementary training. Anthony was always a worry to Jimmy, for "he was far too brave and headstrong to make a successful fighting pilot". His elder gave him such education as time allowed. In May Jimmy had a crash, at Barming by Maidstone, when engine failure gave him the choice between a hop-garden upwind or a small field downwind. He chose the latter and piled up his machine. "I felt very cheap, as I was to blame for flying so low over bad landing country." He had 450 hours to his credit and only a very high grade of pilot would have got off so lightly.

On 13 June he flew to Croydon in a Sopwith Pup to give one of his lectures and arrived just in time to learn that a formation of German bombers had crossed the coast and was heading for London. He shot back to Joyce Green to pick up his Lewis gun and while "we were putting the gun on I could plainly hear the roar of the many engines of the Hun formation which had just passed over".

In accordance with RFC tradition McCudden, alone, went after them. Over Sheppey he had spurred the Pup to 15,000 feet and there he caught a glimpse of over twenty machines, "all with 2-pusher engines". By the time he had come within 500 feet of the rearmost they were twenty miles out to sea and "visions of a long swim entered my mind". He fired three drums at the invaders without effect and turned for home. This experience brought about a change in McCudden's mental attitude. Up till now he had felt no more than the usual regular soldier's fairly neutral view of the enemy, an enemy of King and country who must be destroyed but without rancour. Now: "How insolent these damned Boches did look, absolutely lording the sky above England! I simply hated the Hun more than ever." The raid, in fact, had been not merely a legitimate act of war but an exceedingly brave one, though the RFC could not be expected to look at it quite so dispassionately. McCudden then spent a little time with 56 Squadron at Bekesbourne, near Canterbury, which was uneventful except for one thing. No. 56 was a very fine Squadron and was one of the first to be equipped with the Hispano-engined SE5a. McCudden had found his ideal machine. The SE, with its interrupter-controlled Vickers gun, in addition to a Lewis on the top plane would be to him what the sword Excalibur was to Arthur.

When McCudden came back to France in mid-July 1917 Ball was dead with forty-four victories to his credit, and he had no obvious successor. In the opposing camp the name of power was Manfred von Richtofen, whose Jagdstaffel No. 11 was at the height of its fame. The Baron was not an attractive figure, whatever his skill as a pilot; no man who orders a suitably inscribed cup and presents it to himself every time he shoots down a helpless reconnaissance machine can be considered winning. To cut him down would call for uncommon skill, for like a sensible man he kept in formation, but it was the ambition of every fighter pilot in the RFC.

McCudden, with his new hatred of the enemy, would have been glad of the job but he was not there to fight spectacular duels for the newspapers. He had been sent back to active duty with the object of gaining up-to-date experience before going back to instructing, and that he quietly did. For a week he flew Pups over the Ypres salient with No. 66 Squadron, taking his share in the dog-fighting which now numbered anything up to thirty machines whirling round high above the mud. Then he was attached again to No. 56 and was given an SE. This squadron had an *esprit de corps* all its own, Major Blomfield's orchestra being famous, and it contained some of the finest pilots in France, prominent amongst them being Arthur Rhys-Davids and Cecil Lewis both still short of 20 years of age. Rhys-Davids, who looked like a nice sixth-former, was a tiger in a fight in whom "we had a second Ball, for neither of them knew the word fear and it was largely the splendid example which they set which made the Squadron do so extraordinarily well at a time when, taken collectively, the German morale was at its zenith". He was shot down in October, having well earned his DSO and two MCs.

The rest of July saw McCudden back on Pups, throwing this very manoeuvrable little aeroplane about in rolls, turns, dead-leafs and spins in a way that few cared to do. On one occasion, trying to clear a separated case in his Vickers, he was himself jumped by an unseen enemy and came down with his tail ablaze; on another he took on five Albatros V-strutters with the intention of picking off their leader and then making himself scarce. "As soon as the Hun heard me he started to dive, and I was fool enough to follow a little too far, for in this way I got below the bulk of the Huns, who all opened fire on me with one accord. I at once experienced that strange feeling that one does on these occasions, but I remember saying to myself, 'Now, Jimmy, pull yourself together or you'll be for the sports'." By sheer perfection of flying he threw them off. He put it down, as usual, to luck, adding that "on that occasion my blood-thirstiness outweighed my better judgment. However, all these escapes did me a big lot of good and gave me a lot of confidence and experience for the future." His machine had only been hit twice.

In August 1917 he went back to Joyce Green, but not for long. Pilots of McCudden's quality were badly needed and within a fortnight he was back with No. 56 as a Captain and Flight Commander.

McCudden and the SE5 were suited to each other, each being the best of its kind. On his first day out he shot down an Albatros – one of his pilots, Barlow, accounted for two – and found to his delight that his machine could move and climb faster than anything the enemy could put against it. He subjected every part to minute examination, "for I am a stickler for detail and .. such a thing as having dirty goggles makes all the difference between getting and not getting a Hun". He took his new responsibilities seriously, as a good Regular should. The new pilots were told firmly that the days of the lone ranger were over and that the flight must stick closely to him unless it could not possibly be avoided. The two greenest men were

always made to fly at the back of the five, with rigid instructions that if they were attacked from behind they must
instantly dive underneath the aircraft in front and leave the
rest to him. This sensible course of action reduced casualties
amongst the newcomers and gave them the confidence which
was half the battle. The Squadron cut down a great many
enemy aircraft at uncommonly small loss to itself.

McCudden remained with No. 56 throughout the rest of
1917 and until a few days before the great German offensive of
March in the following year. B Flight had been very good
before he took it over, but under his leadership it attained
something like perfection. His pilots, Barlow, Rhys-Davids,
Muspratt, Coote and Cronyn, were not far behind him in skill
and determination. Of the first two he wrote that "they would
have chased the Huns over to the Russian front if I had let
them" – the news that there was no longer a Russian front
seems to have been kept from them – and of Rhys-Davids that
"if one was ever over the Salient in 1917 and saw an SE5
fighting like Hell amongst a heap of Huns, one would find nine
times out of ten that the SE was flown by Rhys-Davids".
Maurice Baring arranged for Orpen to paint some of them
while there was still time. "Orpen beat McCudden at ping-
pong and arranged to paint portraits of Hoidge and Rhys-
Davids, which he did in the course of time." He also painted
McCudden, looking unusually serious. "Rhys-Davids," wrote
Baring, "had only just left Eton, where he had been Captain of
the School. He was longing for the war to be over so as to go to
Oxford. He told me he always carried a small volume of Blake's
poems in his pocket in case he should come down on the other
side. He also said to me one day: 'The Buddhists have got a
maxim, *Don't be stupid:* that is all that matters in life'."

When McCudden left No. 56 his flight had accounted for
seventy-seven enemy aircraft, with only four casualties of their
own. It was an amazing feat and owed much to his leadership
and tactical skill. His beginnings had made one thing clear to
him. War was not jousting with a chivalrous enemy, even
though Rhys-Davids might have drunk to Richtofen as "Our

most worthy enemy". Flying Corps existed to spy out enemy
movements, to direct guns on to their targets and to drop
bombs on useful places. Fighters existed not to fight fighters,
except incidentally, but to knock down spotters and bombers.
If, to do this, they must mix it with escorts he was willing to
take on all-comers, but it was a secondary business. His concern was not to lead his flight as if it were a cricket team but to
work out how to catch the enemy at a disadvantage, take him
unawares if he could and break off at once if things looked
unpromising. He was a bad hater, almost apologizing for
catching a German two-seater when its attention was elsewhere and reproaching himself bitterly on the one occasion
when he sent an Albatros down in flames.

The score mounted steadily and a blow-by-blow account
would make tedious reading. As the flight always operated as a
body it fell more often than not to the leader to make the actual
kill and McCudden's total rose into the tens, twenties and
thirties. Only once did he and Richtofen come near to a shoot-
out, over Langemarck at the end of September. McCudden
spotted a V-strutter a mile off giving the *coup de grâce* to a Pup
and hurried to join in; by the time he arrived the Pup had hit
the ground and the Albatros was far away. Next day the
German wireless announced that the Baron had "shot down
his sixtieth opponent in aerial battle". He continued until
April 1918 when he himself was bagged either by an Australian
cook with a Lewis gun or by the Canadian Roy Brown. The
argument is still unfinished. McCudden never saw him again.

The other German "kanone" was Werner Voss, who had a
score of forty-odd. B flight met him with two others near
Zonnebeke on 24 September and a mêlée of Homeric quality
followed, McCudden, Mayberry, Hoidge and Rhys-Davids all
diving, zooming and turning like a mob of starlings. Others
joined in and by the time the fight ended there were eleven or
fourteen enemy aircraft milling about the seven SEs. Rhys-
Davids went after a triplane, went off to change his drum and
came back. "Last dive but one. I went for him. He came from
the east. Not quite straight behind, fired from a hundred yards

to 70 and emptied a whole drum. The triplane only turned when 20 yards away. I turned to the right, so did he. Thought situation impossible, and that there would be a collision. I turned left and avoided him. I next saw the triplane at 1500 feet below gliding West. Dived again, opened fire at about 100." McCudden saw the triplane go into a steep descent, hit the ground and "disappear into a thousand fragments, for it seemed to me that it literally went to powder". "I shall never forget my admiration for that German pilot, who single-handed fought seven of us for ten minutes, and also put some bullets through all our machines. His flying was wonderful, his courage magnificent, and in my opinion he is the bravest German airman whom it has been my privilege to see fight." Rhys-Davids, who had shot Voss down, was heard to say, "If only I could have brought him down alive." Four days later Barlow, out on his own, shot down three Germans in as many minutes.

Captain McCudden, between flights, was still the quiet, amiable young man he had always been He never smoked, drank little and although he enjoyed an evening around the piano there was nothing of the rakehell pilot about him. Nothing interested him but flying; having neither home nor family his only outside interest was his young brother Tony, to whom he stood as Bill had once stood to him. Tony, who had been flying DH4s for some months, mostly on bombing missions, had himself just joined an SE squadron and was making a name for courage of the reckless kind. He was a great worry to Jimmy.

The score of No. 56 was mounting. By the end of September it reached 200. On 23 December McCudden alone shot down four, three LVGs and a Rumpler, bringing his own total to thirty. He explained that he had taken a lot of trouble over his engine and in consequence was able to get to 20,000 feet, the height from which the Rumpler operated usually in safety. On 28 December he sent down three of them within thirty minutes. Early in the New Year he destroyed another LVG which put the Squadron total to 250 and that of B Flight to 100, a figure never before achieved by a single flight. No doubt, as with Richtofen, many of McCudden's battles were unequal affairs but he awarded himself no cups. "I hate to shoot a Hun down without him seeing me, for although this is the method in accordance with my doctrine, it is against what little sporting instincts I have left." It was skilful flying, careful maintenance and excellent shooting that had made him the leader amongst the "hired assassins", as they called themselves. With a telescopic sight for the Vickers he held that "400 yards is not extreme range so long as a pilot has his machine guns aligned correctly and intelligently with his sight". Nor had he any sympathy with slackness. The crew of a DFW shot down over Vitry on 24 January "deserved to die, because they had no notion whatever of how to defend themselves, which showed that during their training they must have been slack and lazy and probably liked going to Berlin too often". On 16 February 1918 he again notched up four in a day, bringing his total to fifty.

The shooting down of spotter aircraft had become almost routine but a victory on 18 February gave him far more satisfaction. For months No. 56 had been fighting a private guerrilla with a staffel of Albatrosses led by a pilot known as Green Tail. They had bagged Mayberry, one of B Flight's best pilots, and, after a number of inconclusive scraps, were leading on points when they met over Bourlon Wood at 13,000 feet. McCudden went straight for the leader and got him with the first burst; he then turned and shot down a second. "The pilot of the green-tailed Albatros must have been a very fine fellow, for during my time on the Cambrai front I had many times cause to admire his fighting qualities. I only hope it was my first bullet that killed him." On 5 March, his tally of enemies at fifty-seven, McCudden was sent home, ill and exhausted. Hardly had he arrived at Dover than news came in of the death of young Anthony, shot down over Le Cateau with a score of seven.

On 6 April 1918 Major, as he now was, McCudden went to the Palace to receive from the King a bar to his Military Cross, the DSO and bar and the Victoria Cross. He ended his memoirs with, "I am now in England training the young idea, but my heart is in France amongst the gallant boys who are daily dying, and those who are dead, having given themselves to that most wonderful cause FOR KING AND COUNTRY."

On 9 July 1918 he arrived back in France on his way to take over a Squadron, the renowned No. 60. At Auxi-le-Chateau, as he made to take off in a heavily-loaded plane, the engine failed. Unwisely he attempted to turn back but his machine crashed and killed him. He was just 23.

CHAPTER FOUR

The Top-Scorer

W. A. Bishop

The Grand Hotel, Folkestone, is an hotel no more, but the glassed-in ballroom known to generations as the "monkey-house" remains. It is an unlikely enough place to have introduced to flying the man who in all probability destroyed more enemy aircraft than did any other pilot, but that is where his career began. William Avery Bishop was born on 8 February 1894 at Owen Sound in the Province of Ontario, the son of the county registrar. His boyhood was unremarkable, being that of every Canadian small town child, but it was in early youth that he acquired a skill that never left him. His father was unwise enough to give him a .22 rifle and a promise of 25 cents for every squirrel he managed to shoot, and young Billy soon became a marksman of uncanny skill.

At 19 he went to the Royal Military College at Kingston where he took some pride in his reputation of being the worst cadet ever. The end nearly came at the final examination held in March 1914 when he not merely cheated but handed in his crib notes along with the finished papers. He was sent on leave while the authorities considered what to do with him, and was saved by the war; anybody with an officer's training was an article of value and young Bishop, technically not passed out, was promptly commissioned in an Ontario militia regiment, the Missassauga Horse. He was soon transferred to the Canadian Mounted Rifles and arrived with them at Plymouth on 23 June 1915 after a hair-raising passage amongst the U-boats. From Plymouth the regiment went to the great Canadian camp at Shorncliffe, just outside Folkstone, and Bishop soon took a violent hate to the place. St. Martin's Plain is, admittedly, often wet and windy, but it is not all that bad. Bishop, however, loathed it and took every opportunity to escape to the delights of Folkestone, and especially to those of the Grand Hotel where the best-looking women were to be found. There he poured out his woes to a chance-met RFC pilot who suggested that, if he were as unhappy as he seemed to be, he should give up his horses and turn his thoughts to more up-to-date forms of warfare. The thing to do, he advised, was to get an interview with Lord Hugh Cecil, who in some mysterious fashion was responsible for selecting aspirants to the Flying Corps. Bishop thought well of the idea, took himself off to the Royal Automobile Club, which had been turned into a hostel for Canadian officers, and sought audience.

At Room 613A in the War Office building Lord Hugh settled the destinies of the would-be fliers. He seemed an unlikely man for the job being, at 46, the oldest subaltern in any army and with no military experience behind him. The Cecils had always been politicians and, presumably, centuries at that trade had made them judges of men. It was to be hoped that this was true, for Lord Hugh was a one-man selection board from whose decision there was no appeal. He asked his standard questions about education, horsemanship and addiction to manly games; Bishop gave highly untruthful answers, as did most people, and they appeared to be satisfactory. One thing, however, was certain. There were no immediate vacancies for pilots, but if Bishop liked to become an observer he might take his chance of bettering himself later. Bishop agreed to give it a try. Some years later, when he was famous, he mentioned the interview to Lord Hugh who asserted that, while he had no exact recollection of their meeting, he did recall that Bishop had not struck him as the kind of man he was looking for.

Bishop, certainly, was not the most comfortable of men and he did not fit into the usual pattern. Sholto Douglas, who came to know him quite well, wrote in after years, that "there was something about him that left one feeling that he preferred to live as he fought: in a rather brittle, hard world of his own. He has been described as a lone wolf, but I do not think that any of us came to know him or to understand his motives well enough to be able to be sure about that. He was not a lone wolf in the sense that we applied that description to Albert Ball. With the passing of the years Billy Bishop mellowed in a noticeable way, and when I met him again in the Second World War – he was then an Air Marshal in the Royal Canadian Air Force – he seemed to have become more likeable and companionable". At 21 there was a hardness about him, but he had a hard time ahead of him.

He joined No. 21 Squadron at Netheravon for training on 1 September 1915 and learnt the customary lessons meted out to observers. Christmas was spent in style at the Regent Palace Hotel, "full of people on week-end honeymoons and the grill and the restaurant are full of love-girls and men intent on picking them up", he told his parents. It seems likely that he did not allow this to spoil his Christmas, for female company was never disagreeable to him. Soon afterwards he was in France, observing over the side of the RE7, probably the worst aircraft ever to fly with the RFC. It was described as "a pig – on a windy day a boy on a bicycle can pass it". When burdened with a 500 lb bomb it refused flatly to be parted from the earth. In order to coax it into the air it was necessary to take out most of its armament and No. 21 soon became known as the "Suicide Squadron".

These were amongst the worst days of the war for the RFC, the days of Immelmann and Boelcke, and 21 Squadron had a rough time. It was not the Fokkers, however, that troubled them most; it was the German anti-aircraft artillery, much improved since 1914 and carefully sited under the places where the lumbering RE7s must pass. Bishop's machine was often badly knocked about and he himself suffered a slight head wound. The cold during that winter was lethal and the strain of combining the businesses of observing and sketching with constant glances over the shoulder for Fokkers put a terrible strain on all hands. In his letters Bishop told that "I have the most fantastic luck under fire" and added that his greatest fear was of being taken prisoner. Every airman had a private fear of something: Mannock feared neither man nor devil but he had a horror of being shot down in flames, the fate that eventually was to be his. Bishop put it: "If I can barely live under British discipline, how could I live in a German prison camp?" One cannot avoid the impression that the grumble about discipline was thrust in because it was expected of an independent-minded Colonial boy. He had endured far worse at Kingston and, apart from some necessary and inflexible rules common to all air services, discipline sat pretty lightly on RFC aircrews, at least in their leisure time.

In May 1916 Bishop qualified for UK leave and in his haste to get off the boat at Folkestone – a haste shared by everybody else on board – he slipped and cracked his knee-cap. The damage was bad enough to send him to hospital and there the doctors found that a damaged patella was not all that was wrong with him; cold, overstrain and long periods of hard work had seriously strained his heart. He would have to remain in hospital for some considerable time.

Beyond argument Billy Bishop was a pretty sick man; at a less dangerous stage of the war he would have been taken off flying long since but he had arrived at a season when the RFC was stretched near to breaking and as long as a man could keep in the air he kept there. If the process killed him, that was his misfortune. For Bishop it turned out to be something more like a stroke of luck, for it found him a patroness. When Lady St. Helier visited him in hospital, claiming a slight acquaintance with his father, the name meant nothing at all to him. What he saw was a pleasant-looking woman of about 70 who was well known to the hospital authorities as a constant caller with a particular interest in friendless young men.

Mary St. Helier had, indeed, met the county registrar during a visit to Owen Sound in 1906 when she was on a tour soon after the death of her second husband. She had been born a Stewart-Mackenzie, of the best blood in Scotland, and entered society as the wife of Colonel Stanley, the son of Lord Stanley of Alderley, upon whose death she married the lawyer Francis Jeune, soon ennobled as the first and last Lord St. Helier. On his death in 1905 she scorned widow's weeds and became, as she herself wrote in her *Who's Who* entry, "indefatigable in the service of the poor, and in society is famed for her brilliant art of entertaining". At the age of about 80 she put as recreations "bicycling, riding, skating". Formidable though she was, and daunting to any young man from a lower stratum in the scheme of things, she had a kind heart and the entrée almost everywhere. With the 22-year-old Canadian boy she made an instant hit and Mary St. Helier took a great fancy to him. Soon he began to recover his strength and found himself installed as one of the lodgers in her great house in Portland Place; in no time at all he was addressing her as "Grandma" and she avenged herself by upbraiding him about the state of his hairbrush. Lady St. Helier had long had a special relationship with Lord Hugh Cecil; when Winston Churchill married Miss Hozier, Lord Hugh had been best man and had persuaded Lady St. Helier to hand over 52 Portland Place for the reception, as the Churchills had no house big enough for the purpose. Such claims on gratitude cannot be resisted and between them it was arranged that Bishop should have a spell of home leave in Canada. Before going he met Lord Hugh on the easier footing of a fellow-guest in the same house and put his claims for advancement. He had fairly kept his part of the original bargain, if bargain it could be called, and had served his time as an observer with credit. Now it was up to Lord Hugh to do his part. Lord Hugh, under the basilisk gaze of Lady St. Helier, hurriedly agreed that as soon as Bishop was back in England his wishes should be met. Nepotism should never be cried down, when the right kind of people exercise it. Without the help of the lady, Bishop would probably have gone back to France and shared the fate of No. 21 Squadron.

When he returned from Canada in September the battle of the Somme was half way through its dreadful length. 21 Squadron, still with its awful RE7s, had been wiped out, valiantly and without hope of reprieve trundling to and fro over the line between Albert and Fricourt, an easy prey to the German fighters and anti-aircraft gunners. Pilots and observers such as these were never called "aces" and few people now could name half a dozen of them, but no braver men ever drew on flying boots.

Bishop duly reported himself to Upavon for flying training and it soon became apparent that he was not one of that handful of men who found flying as natural as swimming. Possibly his experience in a machine that needed brute force to move it had not been helpful to him and the instruction at Upavon was not yet of the quality introduced at Smith-Barry's Gosport school. When first invited to return his machine to earth Bishop made a perfect three-point landing; the only fault to be found was that he made it some forty feet above the ground. Some years before the Second World War a very senior Bishop met Goering and the talk, naturally enough, turned to war-time flying. The Reichsmarschall, who had been a decent young pilot before going off the rails, began to brag about his successes. Bishop cut him short with an assertion that he himself had destroyed more allied aircraft than had Goering, by the expedient of wiping off their undercarriages and it was not entirely facetiousness. He never did quite master the art of bringing an aeroplane gently down, for his weakness was always impatience. Once airborne he became another man and few of the trainee-pilots could claim to be his superior. Like Ball and Lewis, he always flew without goggles, insisting that they hampered his view and spoiled his shooting. Only those who have flown an open-cockpit aeroplane can know what this means.

As soon as he had wings on his jacket Bishop was posted to No. 11 Squadron at Northolt where his continual damage to undercarriages made him expensive. For a time it seemed that this flying days were numbered, but he found an ally. Captain

Trygve Gran was a Norwegian who owed his commission in
the RFC to some rule-bending occasioned by the fact that he
had been with Captain Scott on his last expedition to the South
Pole and he had recently served under the famous Jack Scott in
his equally famous No. 60 Squadron. Gran recognized that,
apart from his one failing, Bishop was something out of the
common run of pilots and pleaded energetically for his reten-
tion. Gran's standing demanded respect and, thanks to him,
Bishop was allowed another chance. For a time he was given
the hopeless task of pursuing Zeppelins from the emergency
airfield at Sutton's Farm and after a turn at this he was bidden
to the War Office for orders. There, in a waiting-room, he met
Albert Ball, then the leading fighter pilot with twenty-nine
confirmed victories. Ball, with a DSO and two bars at 20, had
been with 60 Squadron and it seems pretty certain that he told
Bishop of its outstanding excellence.

The friendship of Lord Hugh Cecil was the most valuable
thing an ambitious pilot could possess and it can hardly have
been coincidence that sent Bishop to No. 60, at Izel-le-
Hameau, a few miles to the west of Arras. No better place could
have been found for him; the pilots included a French-
Canadian Major of Pioneers, an Australian, a New Zealander
and two other men from the English-speaking Provinces.
Major Scott was the ideal commanding officer, for he and
Bishop had more in common than might have appeared on the
surface. Scott, a dozen years older than Bishop, had been
before the war a successful barrister in F. E. Smith's chambers
and he was an old friend to Winston Churchill with whom he
had flown a good deal in the pioneer days. Douglas says of him:
"Always cheerful and imperturbable, and charming in his
manner towards everybody, Jack Scott was, for all his spirit,
rather a ham-fisted pilot. He had had a very bad crash earlier in
the war, breaking both his legs, and he could only walk with the
help of sticks; but disabilities were not allowed to stand in his
way. He brought pressure to bear and got himself sent to my
Squadron as a Flight Commander, and whenever the time
came for him to fly he had to be lifted into and out of his

aircraft. We all came to form such a warm admiration for him and the way in which he did things." Scott survived the war and although he was to crash Mr. Churchill more than once their friendship never diminished. At the beginning of his acquaintance with Bishop, however, he came near to having to send him away, for Billy did it again. Breaking up struts and wheels for no obvious reason was a serious offence, and Bishop found himself up in front of the Brigade Commander, the notable General Higgins, who was never called other than "Old Bum and Eyeglass", for he had received a wound usually reckoned disgraceful and was never parted from his monocle. Bishop lied manfully but Higgins would have none of it; a pilot so incompetent must be sent back for further instruction. A mortified young Canadian hung around the Mess for some days and escaped this indignity only because more casualties demanded that he take his place in the flight, however clumsy he might be.

From this moment Bishop's star began to rise. On one of his first patrols, under the leadership of the Australian Alan Binnie, the flight was attacked over Vitry by six of Richtofen's Jagdstaffel No. 11 operating out of Douai. Bishop, flying on the left wing, peeled off on his own, positioned his Nieuport on the broadside of one of the Albatrosses and got in a good burst from his Lewis gun. The German went into a steep dive and Bishop followed him down. It was a common trick amongst German pilots to ape the lapwing and feign injury in the hope of luring an attacker to his own destruction, but Bishop, who had once reckoned to get a squirrel with every shot, had made no mistake. The dive ended in a cloud of dust. Richtofen's men, however, had the better of it, for 60 Squadron lost two for the price of one. Next day Bishop did it again, picking off a second Albatros. The emergence of a possible rival to Ball came at a good moment, for this was April 1917, the month of the Arras battle and one of the worst of the war for the RFC. They exceeded the Germans in numbers but the enemy aircraft were plainly superior and were enjoying a rich harvest. Richtofen was the name of power and he was reckoned invincible; one

squadron at least endured a hundred per cent casualties before
the month was out.

Bishop recked nothing of all this for he was getting his eye in.
He took on Richtofen almost as if it were a personal fight and in
the course of that same month he struck down at least a dozen,
all but two of them single-seater scouts, machines at least as
good as his own. On the terrible Easter Sunday, when Canada
moved inexorably through a snowstorm to the summit of Vimy
Ridge, the former Kingston cadet was looking down on his
countrymen, fighting furiously to give them the cover they
needed. It seems likely that five Albatrosses fell to his gun that
day, though the record gave it as only three. The exploit
brought him a Military Cross.

On 6 May Albert Ball paid Bishop a visit, to discuss a plan
he had long been mulling over. The wasps' nest of Douai
needed burning out and it might be done as a private venture
by the two of them. Ball had been given a roving commission
and was constantly in the air alone carrying out forays of his
own devising. Bishop agreed eagerly and another meeting was
fixed to work out details. Next day Ball was dead, killed
nobody knows quite how, above La Bassee. Bishop mourned
him grievously.

His own life with No. 60 Squadron was not merely a cata-
logue of air fights, for he enjoyed his glass as much as anyone,
was forward in lubricating the Mess piano with champagne
"to improve its tone" and retained an intelligent interest in
women. Charlie's Bar and Les Huitres in Amiens were the
recognized sources of supply for brief encounters of a commercial kind but this was not enough for Bishop. In a chemist's
shop at Amiens he acquired a French mistress of his own,
Ninette by name, and made suitable arrangements. Ninette
seems to have been occupational therapy rather than grand
passion but when they came to part it was on terms of mutual
esteem. Bishop's hardihood was such that when he came to
marry some months later he told his fiancée all about Ninette
and was relieved to find that she adopted a practical attitude to
the business.

The loss of Ball did not put paid to the idea of beating-up a German aerodrome at the hour when visitors were least expected. Douai, with Richtofen himself in residence, was too much for a single-hander to take on but there were others. Estourmel, near Cambrai, for example. Scott readily gave permission and on 1 June Bishop called there. Maurice Baring quotes a letter from some unnamed but well-informed person about what happened. "A certain Corps Commander complained of some machines flying low over its lines. So Bishop, a Canadian pilot, was given a free hand to deal with the matter as he thought best. He went to a Hun aerodrome and there saw the Hun machines all spread out ready, starting their engines. This was very early in the morning. He flew down low as if he were going to land. He shot one mechanic, who was starting an engine, dead, and disposed of that machine. Another, which had just got off, he drove into a tree, where it crashed; a third he brought down a few hundred yards from the Aerodrome. Then he came home. He went down to about 20 feet. Think of the audacity of it." General Trenchard called it "the greatest show of the war" and it won Bishop his Victoria Cross.

As April had been a dreadful month, so June turned into a bumper one with the arrival of the first SE5s. It was especially good for Canada. Raymond Collishaw shot down six Germans in as many days – his eventual total was sixty-eight – soon after Bishop's aerodrome raid. On 8 June fifteen aircraft from No. 60 deliberately put on a display of stunt flying over Epinay to tempt the Germans into making a fight of it but, like prudent men, they preferred to enjoy the performance from the ground. Then Bishop in his turn met with misfortune. On returning from one of his trips around Vimy the German anti-aircraft gunners caught him. He managed to stagger back, bringing his machine down alongside the Arras–St. Pol road, but he was trapped in the wreckage and hung upside down waiting for the flames to start until some passing Tommies cut him free. It was his worst moment of the war.

At the end of August 1917 Bishop, with forty victories behind him, was near to exhaustion. His friends arranged that

he should have a long leave and that he should spend it in
Canada, after which he should go, as an authentic hero, to look
at the progress that the Americans were making in producing
an air force of their own. For six months he left the war behind,
marrying the girl to whom he had become engaged on the
outbreak of war and touring the American camps and factories. What he found there horrified him, for it was plain that
the States had no idea of what they were in for and had not
made a very encouraging start. He did not keep his opinions to
himself and he ran into trouble on his coming back to England
for talking out of turn. He was by then too important a man for
it to worry him.

At the end of May 1918, the period at which a reluctant Mr.
Lloyd George was being compelled to hurry into France every
man and machine that could plug the gaps left by the German
March offensive, Bishop came back to flying, a Major in command of one of the new squadrons. With this he was entirely
content, for the Squadron was equipped with the latest SE5a,
complete with 200 hp Hispano-Suiza engine, the Vickers gun
fed with a distintegrating metal belt and a CC gear enabling it
to fire through the propeller and a top speed of 127 mph. Ball
had introduced him to the SE a year previously, telling him
that it was a fine machine although his personal choice
remained the Nieuport. Bishop was unlucky in his introduc-
tion to his new mount, for the interrupter gear had been
wrongly adjusted and his first trial burst, fired on the ground,
splintered the propeller. A few minutes work on the pulsator
gear put this to rights and Bishop warmed to the improved
version. With this sort of speed and rate of climb there was no
aircraft on the Western Front that could touch a well-handled
SE5a.

His pilots included some colourful characters and three of
them in particular have kept the tale of No. 85 Squadron fresh
for so long as men read books. The Royal Air Force had come
into existence on 1 April and not all its founder-members
owned allegiance to King George V, for it contained a strong
and refreshing dash of President Wilson's young men. Elliott

White Springs was their chronicler and his two companions, Larry Callahan and Mac Grider, had all their doings and sayings recorded for the rest of time. Springs was the son of an immensely rich cotton man from South Carolina who had had a row with his father and gone for a soldier; Grider, from Arkansas, and Callahan, from Chicago, were both recently down from Princeton. On their own showing they had a pleasingly scatological sense of humour and an unquenchable thirst for drinks that does not sound very agreeable; probably distance lent enchantment when Springs put it all into print, for pilots who took aboard liquor at the rate he claims would never have lived to write about it. The trio acquired a house in Berkeley Square where a non-stop party seems to have continued by day and night, broken only by visits to other parties at Murrays and the Grafton Galleries. Sholto Douglas, a regular guest, says rather primly that "the shows in town were enlivened with the attentions that they paid to the young actresses of that time". Surprisingly enough Springs, who got into trouble after the war for advertising ladies' undergarments in a fashion regarded as lubricious, had a Puritan streak in him; visitors to Berkeley Square were given a fair warning that "horizontal refreshments" were not on the menu. With Bishop, now a little cramped by the presence of Mrs. Bishop and her memories of Ninette, they hit it off famously.

At the end of May No. 85 Squadron arrived at a less animating home, the aerodrome near Dunkirk called Petite Synthe, and at once began operations. The RAF was now well on top of the enemy and 85 shared in the general success. Bishop's personal score mounted steadily, for he led his troops into battle and, with the fighting now being done strictly by formations, the right to the *coup de grâce* was his. From a mere forty his kills rose into the sixties, being given a boost when he shot down five enemy aircraft over Ploegsteert in fifteen minutes, a feat without precedent. It was the beginning of the season of the great killings; Captain Trollope knocked down five in the course of one day, a few days later Captain Woollett did precisely the same thing, and during May the RAF accounted for 130 German aircraft.

If this was not bad enough for the German Air Force, the news that the first American squadrons were now operational as integral parts of the US Army cannot have been heartening. As the American pilots and mechanics were withdrawn so other governments began to look afresh at their positions. Australia had formed its own national Flying Corps and a school of thought arose that the dignity of Canada demanded that she do no less. Canadian pilots of the highest quality abounded but one name stood out above the others and was the obvious choice for command of a Canadian Flying Corps. Billy Bishop was made up to Colonel, given command of a Wing in order to widen his experience and No. 85 Squadron was turned over to "Mick" Mannock, under whom it did better than ever. The end of the war came before anyone expected it and the need for a Canadian national force passed with it. Bishop went home, his work done.

Between the wars he went into business, with varying degrees of fortune, retaining 52 Portland Place as his London address for a long time. With the Second World War he returned as an Air Marshal, but once again it was young man's work and his contribution was useful rather than spectacular. There still remain a surprising number of men about the place with a right to the RFC tie, but Bishop's death in 1956 marked the passing of the last of the giants.

CHAPTER FIVE

The Wild Goose Returns

Mick Mannock

Mick Mannock, during his early days, amused himself by playing the stage Irishman, but it does not appear that he ever set eyes on the country that formed him. As a child he was what the Americans call a barrack-rat, the son of a Regular soldier and born to the sound of bugles. His father does not seem to have been a man of any outstanding merit for, although he was the son of a Fleet Street editor, he had enlisted under a false name and it was as Trooper Corringhame of the Greys that he wooed and won the beautiful Julia O'Sullivan of County Cork. Their second son Edward, more often called Mick, was born in Preston Cavalry Barracks at Brighton on 24 May 1887, thus sharing a birthday with Queen Victoria. When Trooper Corringhame's period of Colour service was up he re-enlisted, this time under his real name and in the 5th Dragoon Guards. It was a common enough trick, for a reservist could not rejoin and still draw reserve pay. Possibly Corringhame-Mannock, like a lot of other men, thus managed to get a double source of income.

For six years the family was in India, where Mannock senior served at Meerut under the command of Colonel R. S. Baden-Powell. The Army has always looked after its children and Mick no doubt got the elements of his education there, as the other soldiers' sons did. His father went with the Regiment to South Africa where he seems to have borne himself creditably enough, for he left the Army as a Corporal after the war when he was discharged at the Cavalry Barracks in Canterbury. There, with the family settled in a little house in Military Road, the Corporal marched out, leaving Julia to manage as best she might.

Mrs. Mannock buckled to, and the boys did what they could to help. Patrick, the eldest of four children, got himself a job as a linesman with the National Telephone Company while Mick was put briefly to school. Of necessity he left at the earliest possible moment, for money was badly needed. He worked as a greengrocer's boy, as a barber's assistant and as soon as he was old enough for it Patrick got him into the Telephone Company to be trained in the same job as his own. Julia Mannock was plainly a woman of quality, for Mick adored her; he seems to have adopted her soft Cork manner of speech and to have inherited her Irish character. Even as a poor boy in a Cathedral City life was not bad, for Mick spoke of his cricket and his football, of the Church Lads' Brigade, and of his joining the new Territorial Force. Oddly enough he did not choose any of the combatant units, all of which could have done with recruits, but went into the RAMC, as a medical orderly with the 44th Division Field Ambulance. Promotion must have been quick, for he was a Sergeant within a short time. This may have influenced his choice, for every penny counted and as a RAMC Sergeant, lumping together his bounty and pay for annual camp, he could have picked up a useful sum; far more than he would have come by as a private in the 4th Buffs.

The new job meant a move from Canterbury and Mannock was sent to work in Wellingborough; there he lived with a family named Eyles with whom he became great friends. He kept up correspondence with them for many years and his letters mostly refer to himself as "Pat" "Murphy" or "Paddy", being usually signed with one or other of these names. It was in Wellingborough that he showed interest in politics, for he became an avowed socialist and secretary of the local Labour Party. His Indian years had given Mannock an advantage over most boys of his kind for it had shown him that there was a world outside Kent and he had a strong urge to better himself; there was nothing in him of envy but he had ambitions, possibly strengthened by an idea of making up to Julia something of the suffering she had been caused by his father's defection. He knew a lot about telephone engineering and there were jobs to be had in countries where the invention was now being developed. Constantinople seemed as likely a place as another and to Constantinople he went, helped by a small loan from the Eyles, which he repaid punctiliously.

The Eastern telephone company was glad to have him. It was February 1914 and Turkey, reeling from successive Balkan Wars and political upsets, was not a popular place for the English to work in. Germany was unquestionably the top power, Baron von Wangenheim, the Kaiser's Ambassador, being the most important figure outside the government, and anything English was being cried down. When Turkey entered the war in November the English colony had a very thin time, with internment being followed by near-starvation; when the Turkish attack on the Suez Canal was driven back matters became even worse. Up to this time Mannock had been a good-natured young man with no particular dislikes. Before long he had developed one strong hatred: not for the Turks, but for their German overlords. There is no record of any special incident that affected Mannock's mind but undoubtedly the capital contained a good many of the worst kind of German who would have found quiet amusement in being beastly to the helpless.

All through that winter Mannock remained behind the wire, most of his thoughts being taken up with the matter of survival on a scanty diet of black bread and not much else. He was a fairly tall – if five feet eleven inches be fairly tall – man of naturally lean build and by the spring of 1915 he was becoming skeletal. Then, surprisingly, the cause altered. Early in the year Allied warships had shelled the outer forts of the Dar-

danelles and landed parties to destroy them; on 18 March
came the great bombardment which many people in Constantinople, including the US Ambassador Mr. Morgenthau,
expected to end with the appearance of a Franco-British fleet
off Seraglio Point. At this moment, between the driving-off of
the ships and the Gallipoli landings of 25 April, the Turkish
Government decided to rid itself of useless mouths. Mannock,
a cadaverous 28 with a doubtful left eye, was reckoned one of
them and was put into a train and set back to England. Had
Baron von Wangenheim been able to foresee the future he
would have shot him with his own hand.

At about the time that *River Clyde* was driving her forefoot
into the sand below Sedd-el-Bahr and the Anzacs were jump-
ing ashore from ships' boats off Gaba Tepe, Mick Mannock
arrived home, bent on vengeance. The 44th Division had left
for India but a third-line Field Ambulance remained and he
hastened to join it, though with no intention of staying long. He
was given back his Sergeant's stripes but as soon as he was
heard swearing that he would never lift a finger to save German
wounded medical eyebrows were raised. This was plainly no
place for Mannock. His own view of the matter was the same,
and he applied for a commission in the Royal Engineers,
announcing that he wanted to join a tunnelling company and
"blow the ———s up". As nobody found this reprehensible
and such zeal deserved encouragement he was sent to a cadet
battalion. There the Adjutant interviewed him and asked
casually whether Mick was related to his friend Frank Mannock. Mick's answer, that they were cousins, seemed to surprise him, for Frank – presumably the son of a brother of the
Fleet Street editor – was an urbane character and Mick was
not. "A tall, hard-bitten fellow with more the appearance of a
Colonial than of an Englishman, blue-grey eyes, clean-shaven
face and a rather grim expression." By now it was the late
summer of 1916 and the name of Albert Ball was being heard in
every Mess and pub. Mannock, like any mettlesome man, was
captivated by his feats and the pleasing idea of working in the
claustrophobic atmosphere of a tunnelling company began to

pall. Being a creature of extremes, he decided that the hawk was preferable to the mole and announced that he would like to fly.

It was not difficult to secure permission to try, but there was a stiff medical examination to be passed and those who lived with him knew all about Mannock's left eye. A lot has been written about this, and one must suspect that it was over-done. Astigmatism in the left eye is not, apparently, uncommon. As Mannock was nearly 30 it seems probable that his eyes had got used to each other and later on he had a name for being long-sighted out of the common. Nevertheless, the examination had to follow strict rules and there was nothing perfunctory about it. Mannock, knowing all this perfectly well, thought out a means of working his way through. His most dangerous moment would come when the doctor confronted him with the little white board with lines of black print of varying sizes. There seemed no way of getting a preview of the one to be used; Mannock practised the art of memorizing the letters shown to his good eye for long enough to reel them off again when the turn of the doubtful one came. Very possibly – there is no exact account of what happened – his natural gift for blarney distracted the over-worked man's attention for the necessary seconds. The certainty is that he passed and was sent off to the School of Military Aeronautics at Reading. After six weeks there he moved to Hendon where, at the end of November 1916, he qualified as a pilot on the Maurice Farman Longhorn. Although initially his report said that he was "poor at landing", Mannock was one of those rare men, a natural flier. As these were badly needed in France he was spared the usual period as an observer and went straight to his squadron as a pilot. He had other advantages over the earlier arrivals for his advanced instruction was all given by competent teachers on modern tractor aircraft and he was not obliged to un-learn the heavy-handed ways of the pusher before mastering the newer, faster and handier machines.

For a while he was kept at Joyce Green as part of the defences of London against marauding Gothas – it was there that he first met McCudden – and it was not until the dreadful month of April 1917 that he reported himself to Robert Loraine's No. 40 Squadron. Loraine, as anyone who may have persevered so far will remember, was not over-popular with his young pilots, but Mannock would not hear a word against him. "One of the best," was his verdict in a letter home. As Mannock was much nearer to Loraine in age and had seen much more of the world than had pilots who had recently been schoolboys it may not be all that surprising that they liked each other. Each sometimes had a vile temper and that always makes a bond between men. It was not so much this, however, that warmed Loraine to him as the early demonstration that he had acquired a pilot of exceptional skill. No. 40 was flying Nieuport Scouts and there were several witnesses to Mannock's first exploit who have recorded it. As Sholto Douglas was a distinguished pilot he must speak with the greatest authority. "I was standing with some of my pilots by one of our squadron hangars, and we were watching one of the Nieuports of No. 40 Squadron swooping down on a ground target used for practice firing on the range near the aerodrome. I noticed that the pilot – who was Mannock, although I did not know that at the time – appeared to be diving the Nieuport rather more steeply and fiercely than was usual. As he started to pull out of the dive the lower plane of his aircraft, which was narrower and shorter than the top plane, buckled and fell away. By all the laws that govern such events, that Nieuport should have gone plummeting into the ground; but Mannock, fully aware of what had happened, cooly throttled back his engine and managed, by first-rate flying and supported only by his top plane, to glide into a field alongside our own airfield. He turned over on his back on landing, but he was unhurt. Inexperienced though he was, Mannock showed in that one incident that he was made of the right stuff."

Life for No. 40 Squadron consisted of offensive patrols, sweeps in formation well behind the German lines, seeking out the fighters that were decimating the hapless artillery-spotters. It was exacting work, cold, lack of oxygen at great heights and enemy anti-aircraft fire creating far more dangers for them than did enemy aircraft. As Mannock wrote in his diary, "The Huns clear off invariably when they spot us coming." It was their business to do so, for a pilot earned his pay by knocking down disadvantaged two-seaters, not by demonstrations of mediaeval chivalry. Loraine kept good discipline and his flights stuck tight together, their presence in inexpugnable groups being a better insurance to the BEs than any number of separate single combats would have been. Mannock neither particularly liked nor particularly hated the life. He was often knocked about by anti-aircraft fire and was caught up in a good many of the inconclusive mêlées of the time but, apart from the one display of his flying skill, nothing came his way that did not come to the rest of the Squadron. He suffered, as all did, from the headache that high-flying pilots get, but apart from that he was happy enough. It was an agreeable surprise, he wrote, to find that there were no licensing hours and he could get a whisky and soda at any time and tobacco was plentiful; in fact he never drank much but he was an inveterate pipe-smoker. He flirted shamelessly, as a decent man should, with the French girls and the prettier Irish nurses, but he did not go wenching. Being a tolerable pianist he was useful after dinner and his companions seemed to like him. What worried him most was the fact that he did not seem to be getting anywhere.

It was a kind of slack-water period in the air war. Times were beginning to change, and the death of Ball had ended a short era. Only he had made a big score; every pilot worth his salt wanted to be another Ball but it seemed as if such a performer would never come again. Mannock, in his first month, did succeed in driving down one enemy aircraft out of control but all that he had to show for weeks of work and strain was wear and tear on an always tight-strung nervous system. On 8 May 1917, the day after Ball's death, he was one of a flight of seven that went out to destroy the same number of balloons near Vitry. They flew in at about twenty feet, each picking off his target, and one Nieuport was caught by the guns. It was a notable feat, but his only one. The raggedness of his nerves became manifest, and word went round that Mannock, if not actually "yellow", showed signs of being over-careful in engagements".

It seems likely that Mannock, at this time, was not as popular with other subalterns as writings about him suggest, for not only was he considerably older than they were but he was a different kind of animal. The young pilots, the kind who had staged the "all together, boys!" on Loraine were for the most part public school products whose background and interests did not chime with his. Mannock, the avowed socialist, began with a prejudice against them, for their habits of speech bored him; for their part they saw him as an outsider, pleasant enough but not of the same totem. It was a period of the war when some pilots were under suspicion, often unjustly, of being disinclined and a man who could not be measured in the usual way was inevitably more open to question than those who all came out of the same mould. Mannock's pet hate, apart from Germans, was the Society women whose photographs came regularly into the Mess with the illustrated papers. A picture of the beautiful Lady Bagwash opening a bazaar in aid of our poor, dear wounded was always guaranteed to excite him to paroxysms of rage and he certainly had a class-consciousness lacking in McCudden. It cannot have been helpful, especially as once in a while the lady might have been somebody's aunt.

His lack of success continued, though his dead honesty about claims may have made it seem worse than it was. On 2 June 1917 he "had a scrap, emptied a full drum into a big coloured two-seater at twenty-five yards. Must have riddled the bus, but nothing untoward happened. She put her nose down and went straight." There was seldom time to spare in which to be certain of what happened to one's target and many a man would have staked a claim for this one. His tactics at this stage were still those of Albert Ball, to go in straight and hard without much finesse. Four days later he employed them on a two-seater over Lille, closing to twenty-five yards before opening fire, and there was no doubt about the end of that one. Talk of over-cautiousness began to fall off. Then, on 16 July,

Mannock had a stroke of bad luck. In a flying accident a piece of metal entered his good eye and a small operation became necessary. As this compelled the authorities to send him on leave it was not wholly unfortunate, for Mannock was suffering badly from wear and tear.

He spent the leave in London, mostly at the RFC Club in Bruton Street, and was back with the Squadron early in July. His eye was quite healed, the rest had done him good and Mannock began to score again. On the 12th he shot down another two-seater, this time within the lines, and went to inspect the wreckage. When he saw the remains of the pilot and of his little terrier Mannock lost sight of his hatred and wrote home that "I feel like a murderer". His moods changed quickly; on another occasion, much later, he was not content to bring a machine down but insisted on raking the wreckage with his gun, to the disgust of his companion. More than one man dwelt inside Mick Mannock. A week after destroying the two-seater he had a straight fight with an experienced German pilot, Leutnant von Bartrap, whom he ambushed on the way back from an attempt to puncture a balloon. Mannock, after some minutes of manoeuvring, got him squarely and was well pleased to learn that von Bartrap had suffered nothing worse than a broken arm. Then followed weeks without another kill, even though the Squadron was re-equipped with the SE5a. In December, his score standing at nine, Mannock was posted home.

He underwent a wireless course at Biggin Hill and it was there that he heard of a new fighter squadron, No. 74, being formed. Mannock was determined to get into it and so informed General Henderson, who let him have his way. No. 74 came into existence in the best possible fashion. It had a nucleus of very experienced practitioners, its machines were the latest mark of SE and all its pilots had been schooled together as a training squadron. Instruction now was a thoroughly professional business and there was no longer any question of half-trained boys being sent to France with only a few hours flying behind them to act as Fokker-fodder.

Given half a chance it would soon become a very formidable formation and Mannock was delighted to be promoted Captain and given command of one of its flights.

Most of the big names belonged to men who were splendid fighters but individualists who did not take kindly to the responsibility of looking after others. Mannock went to the other extreme, for it was as a leader that he excelled; not merely as the first man in the fight but as a wise and usually patient teacher of the men who must themselves be the next generation of commanders. The chip on his shoulder contracted with his rise in rank and it was discovered that he lectured extremely well. He had had quite a lot of speaking practice in the mock-parliaments of his early socialist days but it seemed wiser not to make too much of this. One copy-book heading he drummed into all his young men. "Always above: seldom on the same level: never underneath." The Ball gambit was strictly for the experts.

Taken in the round, the SE5a was probably the best fighting aeroplane produced by either side during the war, but the German designers had not been idle and there was never a moment when an SE pilot could pitch into anything he saw with a light heart. The SE was very fast, but it had limitations. Mannock spoke of them with some firmness. Take the Albatros or Halberstadt any way you please, for the SE can always outfight them unless the pilot is outstandingly good. The Fokker DV11, a machine so respected that the Armistice agreement contained a special clause demanding the immediate handing-over of all of them, was another matter. It was marginally slower than the SE but could turn inside it; therefore do not mill around in circles, but attack from above and zoom straight up again was his counsel. Most dangerous of all was the Fokker Triplane. It looked slightly comical, but it carried two Spandaus and it climbed like a lift. "Don't ever attempt to dog-fight a Triplane on anything like equal terms as regards height, otherwise he will get on your tail and stay there until he shoots you down. Take my advice, if you ever do get into such an unfortunate position, put your aircraft into a vertical bank, hold the stick tight into your stomack, keep your engine full on and pray hard. When the Hun has got tired of trying to shoot you down from one position he will try another. Here is your chance, and you'll have to snap it up with alacrity. As soon as your opponent commences to manoeuvre for the next position you must put on full bottom rudder, do one and a half turns of a spin, then run for home like hell, kicking your rudder hard from side to side in order to make shooting more difficult for the enemy, but still praying hard." Two of No. 74's pilots have left it on record that they owed their lives to this exact and practical instruction.

His lectures contained much more of the essence of his own experience. "Scouts must be attacked from above, two-seaters beneath their tails. Hold your fire until within a hundred yards; the closer the better. Be careful of a Hun who fires in short bursts. If he fires long bursts at you he is frightened and probably a beginner. Fight him like hell; he should be easy meat." Gunnery, he insisted, was of far greater importance than fancy flying. For himself he developed and practised a special form of it suitable only to the master hand. Harry Hawker had specialized in the crab-shot but since Richtofen had taken his scalp the use of this had lapsed. Mannock improved on it. First he ascertained where every known German two-seater had its blind spot, usually somewhere abaft the beam. From there, coming in at an oblique angle, it was possible to fire bursts ahead of the engine, with the result that the German would fly into the stream of bullets as a pheasant flies into the pattern thrown by a 12-bore. The deflection shot, when used by a marksman of Mannock's quality, seldom failed to come off.

Fortified with all this learning, No. 74 set off for France brimful of confidence. The pilots were the usual Anglo-Saxon miscellany, including two Canadians (Atkinson and Clements), two South Africans, ("Swazi" Howe from Bremersdorp, and VanIra) and a solitary American named Skeddon. The Commanding Officer was a New Zealander, "Grid" Caldwell, of whom it has been said that he would have been amongst the top-scorers had he not been such a rotten shot. He and Mannock soon became inseparable. The Squadron arrived in France at the end of the first week of the German March offensive of 1918 and went to work immediately. On its first offensive patrol it shot down five for the loss of one and with such confidence added to existing skill it became a fighting-machine of great power.

Mannock suffered from no romantic ideas about chivalry, and he had no illusions about the Baron Manfred von Richtofen. When the news came in that he had been killed Mannock was delighted and made no attempt to suggest anything else. A nuisance had been abated and there was no more to be said, beyond: "The swine is better dead". He himself was now coming on form, and that was far more important. He liked his Wing Commander, the South African Van Ryneveld, he was devoted to Caldwell, with whom he enjoyed many of the hunts called joy-flights, and his young men adored him. The Mess was a happy one, with constant battles between the native British and the coloured troops – everybody else – after dinner and many a cheerful evening was passed at "George Robey's" in St. Omer. To the youngsters Mannock behaved as a big brother, not merely showing them the ropes but taking them on joy-flights to instil confidence. He was a generous man, caring less than most for decorations and the like. When he wrote to Eyles describing one battle he added that "I gave one or two to the Flight to buck them up." The savage streak was still there, however, coming to the surface whenever he thought that a man might not be giving everything. If a pilot dropped out of formation on the excuse of engine trouble, Mannock personally inspected the engine; if he was not totally satisfied, the victim was flayed with accusations of something like cowardice. When one wretched youth arrived from the pilots' pool and admitted that he did not think he could face combat in the air Mannock had his wings torn off by a member of the Flight and replaced with a yellow patch, to be worn until he could be sent away. The good men thoroughly approved.

Mannock is fortunate in his biographer, for Ira Jones was a

notable pilot in his Squadron and had the ability to write. He tells of the man with whom he flew daily. "Fearless, ferocious and cunning . . . as an individual a killer, as a patrol leader a schemer and a fox." There was nothing much wrong with his eyesight, for few men saw more keenly and never once was his Flight caught bending. "During patrols he not only mystified and surprised the enemy but also the formation he led. Once over the lines he would commence flying in a never-ending series of zig-zags, never straight for more than a few seconds . . . As he tilted his machine from side to side he scanned the sky above and below with the eye of an eagle. Suddenly his machine would rock violently, a signal that he had seen the enemy . . . a quick half-roll and there beneath him would be the enemy flying serenely along, the result a complete surprise." Mick always took the leader, the others, from a V formation with about fifty yards between machines, diving and zooming in order to keep the initiative. Height, Mannock preached, was victory, as the weather-gauge had been to sailing ships. The Squadron's score, mostly made by Mannock himself, roared upwards. On 24 May came his DSO; within a fortnight a Bar joined it. His Military Cross had come some time ago.

Jones tells of a typical formation-fight, the one of 21 May. "In his first fight (of the day) which commenced at 12,000 feet there were six Pfalz scouts flying east from Kemmel Hill. One he shot to pieces after firing a long burst from directly behind and above; another he crashed; it spun into the ground after it had been hit by a deflection shot; the other, a silver bird, he had a fine set-to with while his patrol watched the Master at work. First they waltzed round each other like a couple of turkeycocks, Mick being tight on his adversary's tail. Then the Pfalz half-rolled and fell a few hundred feet beneath him. Mick followed, firing as soon as he got in position. The Hun then looped, Mick looped too, coming out behind and above his opponent and firing short bursts. The Pfalz then spun, and Mick spun also, firing as he spun. The Hun eventually pulled out; Mick was fast on his tail. They were down to 4,000 feet.

The Henri Farman Reconnaissance machine (1914) with the pilot on top and the observer with his machine gun slung underneath. On November 2nd Major Robert Loraine, MC (D'Artagnan With Wings), climbed from the under-carriage to the top in mid air when his pilot Montray-Reid was shot.

Lieutenant A. P. F. Rhys Davids, DSO, MC (1897–1917).

Captain Albert Ball, VC, DSO, MC (Robin Hood).

Major J. B. Mc (The Regular).

Captain W. A. Bishop, VC, DSO, MC (The Top-Scorer), taken on 6th August, 1917 by which time he had brought down 37 German aeroplanes.

August 10th, 1910, the Wonder Ace Robert Loraine is cheered off by an admiring Edwardian crowd at Rhos-on-Sea.

O (etc) Major E. Mannock, VC (The Wild Goose). Captain Eddie Rickenbacker (The Yankee Racer).

Wing-Commander C. R. Samson, DSO (The Last Elizabethan), starting out on a flight in his Nieuport Scout from No. 3 Squadron's aerodrome at Tenedos.

Major R. Lufbery.

Group photograph of some of the pilots of the original Forty Squadron, Major Robert Loraine, MC (seated centre); on his right Captain D. O. Mulholland (seated); between them (standing) Lieutenant C. O. Usborne, "The Gadget King," taken at Gosport before leaving for France, August 16th.

The Ansaldo S.V.A. Scout, 1917; an Italian fighting scout which was used as an air racer after the War (Wing span 29′ 8″)

The Charming American Wonder Ace Captain E. V. Rickenbacker with his Spad DX III, 220 hp Hispano-Suiza engine. Single seat fighting scout.

This sad and dramatic photograph shows the dead Lieutenant Quentin Roosevelt, son of President Roosevelt, lying beside his crashed Nieuport 28. He belonged to the 95th Pursuit Squadron AEF and he is buried on this very spot where he fell, which today is marked by a star set in a stone circle.

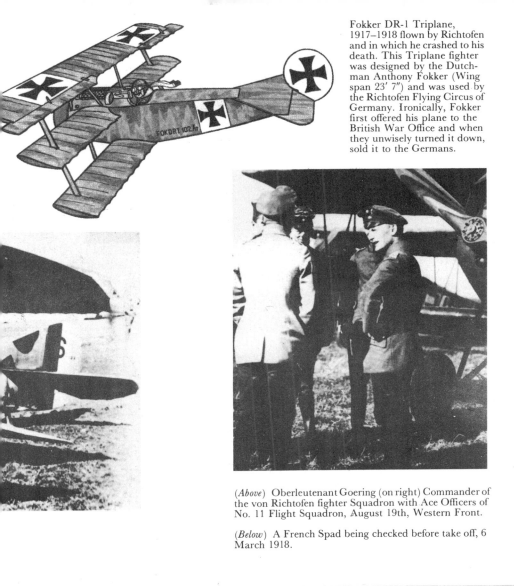

Fokker DR-1 Triplane, 1917–1918 flown by Richtofen and in which he crashed to his death. This Triplane fighter was designed by the Dutchman Anthony Fokker (Wing span 23' 7") and was used by the Richtofen Flying Circus of Germany. Ironically, Fokker first offered his plane to the British War Office and when they unwisely turned it down, sold it to the Germans.

(*Above*) Oberleutenant Goering (on right) Commander of the von Richtofen fighter Squadron with Ace Officers of No. 11 Flight Squadron, August 19th, Western Front.

(*Below*) A French Spad being checked before take off, 6 March 1918.

The Intrepid Commander C. R. Samson (The Last Elizabethan) about to start on one of his daring excursions over the Turkish Line in his Nieuport Scout.

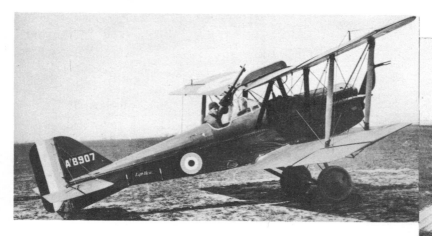

Captain Albert Ball (Robin Hood) in the cockpit of his SE5 Biplane. 150 hp Hispano-Suiza low geared engine. This was an early production aircraft with a semi-enclosed cockpit.

The Sopwith F1 Camel. 130 hp. Clerget 9-Bc engine. Single seating fighting scout. The slots in the engine assisted cooling. This was Major Baker's aircraft.

This aerial photograph is the more remarkable as air-to-air shots of First World War aircraft are extremely rare. It shows an FE2b in flight over England. This aircraft was designed by the Royal Aircraft Factory and proved its worth, in combating the Fokker menace.

(*Below*) The British SE5a was one of the finest aircraft ever built.

The famous FE2 Biplane. 70 hp with Renault engine, ¾ view, taken on 24th September, 1913.

The remarkable and beautiful Felixstowe Fury Fighting Boat, otherwise known as The Porte Baby was the last word in flying boats and its design made possible the first Transatlantic flight in 1919 of the American NC4 Raft whose construction it inspired.

The Handley-Page 0/400 (2 × 275 hp Rolls Royce Eagle engines). This heavy bomber was originally designed for bombing Berlin. It was used by Ross Smith in beating up the Turks in Wadi Fara.

The Pfalz now started twisting and turning, a sure sign of wind-up. After a short burst close up, Mick administered the *coup de grâce* and the poor old fellow went down headlong and crashed." When they had all returned home Mannock gave a detailed explanation of precisely what he had done and how it could have been done better. Five days after that the Squadron took part in one of the biggest dog-fights seen on the Western Front. By arrangement, its 18 SEs joined forces with a dozen Bristol Fighters from No. 20 Squadron and the whole body set out looking for trouble. They soon found it, for the German squadrons, with Richtofen to avenge, were as anxious as the RFC to fight it out. A mixed formation of forty, Pfalzes, Tri-planes and Albatrosses, bore down on them and for a full ten minutes the scene from below resembled the autumnal masses of starlings wheeling and diving in search of food. There was no room for any refinement of flying; it was every man for himself, and the risk of death by collision was as great as that of death by gunfire. Oddly enough nobody was seriously hurt and, with ammunition running low, both sides drew off.

Men under the excitement of battle can endure stresses of mind and body beyond ordinary understanding, but sooner or later Nature always presents the bill. By the end of May it was being prepared for Mannock. His life had become hectic and it could not be long continued in this fashion. It had become a habit with him after every successful patrol to make a signal to the Flight inviting his pilots to land in any manner they pleased; aircraft looped, side-slipped or dived according to the whim of the individual and landing was more after the style of a circus than of a disciplined unit. Mannock said that he did it to cheer up the air mechanics, who worked hard though getting little fun out of life, but it killed the unlucky American, Sked-don. On coming back from a fight and seeing the leader's Very light signal he looped joyously over the hangars, not knowing that his machine had been well peppered. The top plane snapped and he crashed from only a few feet. This sobered everybody up for a moment but it did not last. In accordance with custom they sang, Mannock leading, "For He

Was A Jolly Good Fellow" and returned to business. As the
score of No. 74 mounted the most important thing seemed to be
to get ahead of No. 56. Mannock, who had great respect for
McCudden, wrote that he was determined "to beat old Mac's
record or die in the attempt". His private nightmare was the
possibility of going down in flames and it was common know-
lege that he always carried a revolver for the express purpose of
blowing out his brains before the fire took hold of him. His
habit of crying: "Sizzle, sizzle, wonk!" whenever some
unhappy German had hit the ground in a stream of fire was
known to be only his way of covering up the horror he really
felt. It does not seem very delicious now, but it ill becomes
those who have not endured the sort of thing that was a pilot's
lot to criticize too harshly.

By the last days of May there was no concealing the fact that
Mannock's nerves were worn ragged. His eyes appeared sun-
ken and bloodshot, his thin frame was almost emaciated and he
began to crash his machine far too often. At this point in the
war there was no need for a single gladiator, however successful, to be kept flying until he got himself killed, and at the
beginning of June he was sent home on leave. Before he went
No. 74 had marked up a hundred victories and was ahead of
No. 56; by the Armistice its score was 148 enemy aircraft
destroyed, ninety driven down and its own loss only fifteen.
The record still stands.

On 18 June Mannock was promoted Major and given
Bishop's new No. 85. It was a popular move for though there
was little to choose between them as fighter pilots Mannock
was generally reckoned the better commander. The American
Musketeers, Springs, Callahan and Grider, took to him at once
and with Larry Callahan in particular he struck up a strong
friendship. Callahan wrote of it later. "He was determined to
win. He hated the Huns and wanted to kill all of them. He
wasn't interested in just killing them himself. He wanted a lot
of them killed, so he trained us how to do it. That was why, on
several occasions, Mannock made way for a new pilot to come
in and finish off an enemy aircraft that he had already winged.

It was to give the new boy confidence." Mannock hated as only a dedicated socialist can hate; if there was any room for increase in his feeling it came with the news of McCudden's death. Jimmy McCudden had, in fact, been killed by a rare moment of carelessness on his own part, but Mannock's mood was theatrical. He was "going to avenge poor old Mac."

If there is a place for vengeance in war the Royal Air Force had exacted it in full. The month of July alone saw the shooting down of 170 enemy aircraft and thirty-four balloons for a loss of ninety machines. For Mannock it was still not enough; only with the destruction of the last enemy would his restless spirit be satisfied. No. 85 had some very fine pilots, including a young New Zealander called "Maori" Coningham of whom more would be heard in another generation, and they were as anxious to learn as Mannock was willing to teach. His usual morning greeting to the Squadron – which often flew as a complete entity – did nothing to suggest blood-lust; "All tickets, please. Pass right down the lift. Come on, Gentlemen, please; take your seats for the grand finale." It came now almost automatically and without thinking.

The grand finale was indeed approaching, for the German armies had shot their bolt and the brilliant little Australian battle at Hamel on 4 July showed the way the pendulum was swinging. The Royal Air Force and the Australian Flying Corps – between them twice as strong as the French Air Service – ruled the sky and the Americans were becoming more effective with every day that passed. It was not in the German nature to give in without fighting to the last and good formations still existed in sufficient numbers to dispute sovereignty. These were the best days of Hermann Goering, the heir to Richtofen, who with many like-minded men was willing to pull down Valhalla and die in the ruins. On 18 July Mangin's tanks burst out of the forest and the last, hard battles began.

Mannock had now long passed McCudden and was after the title claimed by "old Richtofen", but he did not allow it to interfere with the bringing on of his young men. Donald Inglis, another New Zealander, had not had much luck so far and

Mannock decided to give him the usual personal encouragement. "You haven't got a Hun yet, Inglis, have you?" His "No,
Sir!" was followed by an invitation to make good the defi-
ciency. On the morning of 26 July 1918 they set off together;
there was some delay as Inglis had trouble with his elevator but
they were off in the early dawn, over the German lines by
Laventie. A two-seater obligingly presented itself and Mannock gave it a few short bursts, followed by a signal to Inglis to
come in and finish it off. Whilst Inglis was carrying out his
lesson they lost a good deal of height and drifted down to a few
hundred feet. Inglis took his man whilst the Master stood by
and it was a little while before he was free to look about him.
What he saw froze him with horror. Flame was coming from
Mannock's engine and tongues of fire were beginning to lick
around the linen covering of the fuselage; the SE was falling out
of the sky and Inglis, unbelieving, saw it hit the ground in a
roaring pillar of smoke; then it blew up, pilot, plane and
everything disintegrating before his eyes. Inglis flew back
alone, only capable of babbling incoherently that "the bloody
bastards have got my Major". Nothing of Mannock was ever
found. No. 85 hoped that he had had time to shoot himself
before the flames roasted him.

Larry Callahan mourned him as much as any, for they had
often flown together. "He would always be the low man, not
the high man: that's where I always admired Mannock. He
was always low and I knew it because I was with him. When a
bunch of Huns came along he would goad them into attacking
him while the rest of the boys were off in the distance, waiting.
It worked magnificently. Mannock was such a hell of a fighter
and such a good shot that he could afford to get himself into the
worst position and still shoot his way out. He was a highly
imaginative pilot, and the best shot that I ever saw in my life."
Sholto Douglas, commanding the sister Squadron No. 84, was
more cautious. "Mannock's trap was not one that I felt I could
place any faith in myself, so we in No. 84 Squadron proceeded
along the more orthodox lines of McCudden's strict formation
flying."

His official score was seventy-three: Ira Jones, who ought to have known, put the probable one at ninety-eight. It is not a matter of the first importance. At the end of the war the King conferred a posthumous VC. Corporal Corringhame-Mannock surfaced and arrived to claim it. Though there was nothing to bury, his memory is kept green in Canterbury by a block of flats where the Mannock cottage used to be and by a memorial in the cathedral where an annual service is held.

Few of the biggest men died in straight combat. McCudden was killed in an accident, as were Oswald Boelcke and, probably, Immelmann. Ball, Mannock and, most likely, Richtofen were caught by ground fire. When Arthur Rhys-Davids shot down Werner Voss it was the only jousting death of them all. A few months later the whole business had gone the way of the armoured knight and the sailing ship.

CHAPTER SIX

The Cabinet Minister

Auberon Lucas

A number of good soldiers, their occupation gone, have turned politician; quite a few are operational today. There has been less traffic in the opposite direction, for such useful qualities as ambition, vanity, and deviousness are insufficiently valued in the armed services. Exceptions, of course, have been known. For example, in August 1914 Mr. Wedgwood Benn, Member for the St. George's Division of Tower Hamlets, needed little time to decide where his duty lay; he left the House and joined his Yeomanry regiment. After service in Egypt and the Gallipoli peninsula he found himself, at the age of nearly 40, flying as one of Samson's observers from HMS *Ben-my-Chree* and was sunk with her off Castelorizo in January 1917. Undeterred by this, he qualified as a seaplane pilot, performed prodigies of valour on the Italian front and in due time returned to the Commons weighted down with well-earned decorations. Mr. Asquith's Minister of Agriculture did not come back. All of him that could die lies buried near Bapaume.

Auberon Thomas Herbert was born in 1876, heir to great possessions. He was a most attractive character, outstanding even amongst the splendid young men of the late Victorian age. From Bedford Grammar School he went up to Balliol where his fine physique put him in the first rank of the athletes;

for two years, 1898 and 1899, he rowed No. 7 in the Oxford boat but he was far from being dedicated to organized sport. John Buchan, a life-long friend, left an account of him. "Bron had uncommonly little of the ordinary sportsman about him, being a gipsy. Far better than the ritual of games he loved his own private adventures in by-ways of the countryside. He had an astonishing knowledge of birds and beasts and all wild things. Most of his friends were fine scholars but he did not essay the thorny path of academic honours, having better things to think about." Elsewhere in the same writing Buchan tells that "I have never known a more whole-hearted, hard-bitten nomad than Bron. Nomad, indeed, is not the word, for he did not crave travel and change; a Hampshire meadow gave him all that he wanted. But he was a gipsy to the core of his being, a creature of the wayside camp, wood-smoke and the smell of earth." He loved poetry, had a passion for music, "was most pleasant to look at, and most gentle and courteous in manner". Wanted or not, travel and change were awaiting him when he came down.

As soon as the South African war began, Herbert though uninterested in military matters decided that he must see it. The first chance of getting there came with an offer from *The Times* that he should be their correspondent. He enjoyed his work enormously, writing to Buchan of the beauty of the country and of the good luck that had taken him to such a place. The luck soon ran out. One day he went too far forward during an action and a sharp-eyed Boer put a bullet through his foot. If that were not bad luck enough, worse was to come, for the field hospital was not of the best and the wound was sadly mistreated. Herbert came home but it was too late for the best London surgeons to save the leg; it was amputated below the knee.

For many months he was seriously ill and his friends, Maurice Baring and Buchan amongst them, concluded that his out-of-door life was finished at 24. Very soon they realized their error. "He behaved," says Buchan, "as if nothing at all had happened, and went on with the life he loved. It cannot have been an easy job, but he never showed the strain of it. He was just as fine a sportsman as before and his high spirits were, if anything, more infectious . . . Soon he was scampering about in the New Forest, and hunting, and playing tennis, and stalking on some of the roughest hills in Scotland. He must have had bad hours, but he kept his head high to his friends." This sounds a considerable understatement.

In 1905 his uncle, the last Earl Cowper, died, leaving Auberon heir to the Baronies of Lucas and Dingwall, together with several great houses. "He got them off his hands as fast as he could, for the only place he really cared for was his home at Picket Post in the New Forest . . for he was still the gipsy, careless of a sedentary world and with all the belongings he needed in his wallet." He was not, however, allowed to escape the consequences of birth and possessions so easily. Herbert had never been enchanted by party politics but he came of a Whig house and by 1906 the Liberals were in power. That power was inexpugnable in the lower House but the Lords were another matter and Baron Lucas found himself under strong obligations to take his seat there and become a pillar of his party. Being one of the few liberal peers of any perceptible quality he was soon marked out for office and, to begin with, he was made private secretary to Mr. Haldane, the new Secretary for War. Haldane was, in the opinion of Sir Douglas Haig, the greatest War Minister the country had ever had and it is hard to find his equal. His intellect was massive, like Lucas, he was a dedicated bachelor and the two men hit it off well together. In 1908 Lucas became Under-Secretary for War; three years later he was Under-Secretary for the Colonies, of which he knew nothing, but only remained there for a matter of months before being transferred to a department nearer to his heart as Parliamentary Secretary to the Board of Agriculture. He was made a Privy Councillor in 1912 and two years later he became Minister in his own right, still in Agriculture. He was not a good speaker but even his opponents could not help liking him and wishing him well.

In August 1914, like so many others, he had an agonizing

choice to make. He held a commission in his county Yeomanry but he had lately had a bad fall while steeple-chasing and the Army did not look like wanting him. Thus he remained, a spectator doing work within the capacity of any dotard, while great armies came to grips. It was the new dimension of warfare that caught his imagination; Maurice Baring, his exact contemporary at 38, had gone early to France with a subaltern's commission in the Intelligence Corps and some sort of appointment at RFC headquarters. Baring, once he had learned to roll his puttees, found time to write and keep his friend informed about the exciting life the first squadrons were having; Lucas was sick at heart but never allowed it to be seen. So long as the Liberal government endured he stayed at his desk, but the coming of the Coalition freed him from obligation to remain there any longer. Nepotism may not be, as Jacky Fisher said, the secret of efficiency, but it is not always reprehensible. Suitably employed, it got a wooden-legged Cabinet Minister in his 40th year into the double-breasted jacket of the Royal Flying Corps.

At Gosport Flying School the happiest man amongst the undergraduate-aged pupils was Second Lieutenant The Rt. Hon The Baron Lucas and Dingwall, PC. His excellent eye and steady nerve, added to the fact that a dozen years of life seemed to have dropped away from him, made him just the kind of material his instructors prayed for. His wooden leg, when anybody remembered its existence, seemed to be taken for granted. He obtained his wings with almost contemptuous ease and was posted to a squadron in Egypt. Once there, at the time when an army was clinging to the edges of the Gallipoli peninsula by its finger- and toe-nails, he flew a good deal but details are sparse. Buchan tells of stories coming back of "crashes in the desert many miles from help and such like". Maurice Baring adds a little. Lucas had written from Gosport that "it was not only like going back to a private school but to a foreign one" and had kept up the correspondence; he had, apparently, "taken part in some long distance raids and had one bad crash in the desert".

Egypt was well enough for gaining experience but it was a
back-water and Lucas had set his heart upon becoming one of
the pilots who served Baring's chief, General Trenchard. In
the spring of 1916 he worked his way home, though only to a
training establishment at Dover as an instructor. It was exciting enough, for one of his pupils soon crashed their dual-
controlled machine and was killed; Lucas was lucky not to go
the same way. Buchan met him at a party – "almost the last
given by Count Benckendorff at the Russian Embassy" – some
time in May 1916. "He was a picture of weather-beaten health,
but I noticed that his eyes were different. They had become
more deeply set, as happens to airmen, and also they had lost
their puzzled look. He had found something for which he had
long been seeking. Up in the clouds he had come to his own,
and discovered the secret of life." The authorities tempted him
to stay at home with offers of command of a squadron, but
Auberon Lucas would have none of it. He had joined the RFC
to fight, and fight he would. By the same token it was not right
that he should command men simply because he was a Peer
and a former Minister. First he must have experience of the
ways of the Western Front. He accepted command of a Flight
of FE2bs with No. 22 Squadron as a step on the way to higher
things. Half way through the battle of the Somme he was given
his way.

For the last weeks of his life Lucas was amongst friends. His
base was at Bertangles, alongside the road between Amiens
and Doullens, with Baring hard by at RFC headquarters and
Buchan a few miles away at Beauquesnes. Baring, who saw
most of him, wrote of it: "These last weeks in France were,
perhaps, the happiest of his life. He was an undergraduate once
more and an active soldier, as active, as athletic in the air as he
had ever been on the ground. His youth had been given back to
him with interest, and for his disabilities he had received a
glorious compensation. Apart from his work and his keenness
and whole-hearted interest in the war, in his Squadron, in his
mechanics and in his machine, he enjoyed himself with all the
great gift of enjoyment and fund of gaiety with which he had

enjoyed everything else in his life; his houses, his fishing, his pony-hunts, his steeplechases, his horses, his pictures, his dinner-parties, the performances of the Follies, or, long ago, the days whether of strenuous rowing or idle punting on the river at Oxford and the musical supper-parties at King Edward Street . . . They could not keep him out of the air."

Buchan takes up the story. "The concluding days of October and the first week of November were full of strong gales from the south-west which gravely hampered our flying, for our machines drifted too far over the enemy lines, and had to fight their way back slowly against a head wind. It was an eery season on the bleak Picardy downs, scourged and winnowed by blasts, with the noise of the guns from the front line coming fitfully in the pauses like the swell of breakers on a coast. One evening, I remember, I rode over to have tea with Bron, when the west was crimson with sunset and above me huge clouds were scudding before the gale. They were, for the most part, ragged and tawny, like wild horses, but before them went a white horse, the leader of the unearthly cavalry. It seemed to me that I was looking at a ride of Valkyries, the Shield Maids of Odin hasting eastwards to the battle-front to choose the dead for Valhalla. Two days later Maurice came to me and told me that Bron was missing."

Politicians joining military units as combatants are inevitably objects of suspicion. Even Major Churchill, with respectable credentials as an ex-Regular, found the Grenadier Guards inclined to draw in their skirts as he passed. Auberon Lucas, however, seems to have been better received. His Wing Commander told Baring that "he was too much of a tiger", his Squadron Commander adding that he was "an air-hog". His last fight came on 3 November, the first fine day for weeks and one taken up with activity by both sides making up lost time. The Army commander badly needed to know what the German Army had been doing during the gales; the German Air Service was equally determined that he should stay in the dark. It would have been useless to rely on the lumbering defenceless BE2cs which would have been knocked down like skittles. The

FE, with its big Rolls-Royce engine, was a good compromise, stable enough to take photographs but capable of putting up a fight against most comers.

Lucas took off at the head of his Flight, the leader's ribbon streaming out between the struts. Somewhere over the Arras–Bapaume road the Albatrosses were waiting for them, high above and with the wind behind. Three picked out the leader and tore down on him, their Spandaus ripping away wood and canvas before the British pilots knew they were there. Lucas fought like the tiger he had been called, turning, diving, and climbing again to get at his tormentors, but the odds were too great. One bullet tore into his leg, another pierced his head; that stable aeroplane the FE2b remained on an even – or fairly even – keel long enough to enable the observer, Lieutenant Anderson, to clamber out of his own cockpit into that of his dying pilot and to bring them down to earth, a feat that makes the blood run cold even in the telling.

"Five of our aeroplanes were shot down during the day, three of them from a photographic-reconnaissance formation of No. 22 Squadron led by Captain Lord Lucas," says the Official History. "He never regained consciousness and died the same day."

Auberon Lucas was not an "ace" in the sense that men like Ball, McCudden and Mannock were "aces", but his claim to remembrance is as strong as any. He could honourably have avoided any service at all or have compromised with his conscience by allowing the top men in the RFC to have their way and shunt him into some job that would have been respectable but safe. All this he disdained to do, holding it to be the duty of any man not entirely disabled to fight and, at need, to die fighting. Buchan drew on his last battle to contrive the end of Pieter Pienaar who, despite a ruined leg, rammed his machine into an enemy to deny him sight of the thinness of a British army on the ground. Had Auberon Lucas not done what he did and been remembered for it, the chances are that Douglas Bader would be remembered only by his friends and as a young man who met early with misfortune and never flew again.

The last word must be with Mr. Churchill. He tells of the first Cabinet meeting after the declaration of war and how he found there two new faces, both well known to him. One was Lord Kitchener, the other the new Minister of Agriculture. "Both these two men were marked for death at the hands of the enemy, the young Minister grappling with his adversary in the high air, the old Field Marshal choking in the icy sea. I wonder what the twenty politicians round the table would have felt had they been told that the prosaic British Cabinet was itself to be decimated in the war they had just declared." There have been some politicians who were neither ambitious, vain, nor devious.

CHAPTER SEVEN

The Last Elizabethan

C. R. Samson

In the Kunsthistorisches museum at Vienna is a miniature by Hilliard of the Young Francis Drake. Remove his ruff, add a leather flying helmet but leave the small neat beard and you are looking at the young Charles Rumney Samson, Royal Navy, in about the year 1911. Nor is the resemblance the only thing common to the two men. The career and exploits of Air Commodore Samson, as he eventually became, suggest that there may be something in the theory of transmigration of souls.

His background and antecedents give no clue as to how he emerged as the undoubted ancestor of all naval airmen, for he was born in Manchester in 1883, the second son of a prosperous solicitor with no family tradition of adventure even in its mildest form.

His family numbered four brothers and it was not of great importance when Charles looked bleakly on the aridities of the law of real property and the farrago of nonsense called the Rules of the Supreme Court. From the very beginning he was certain in his mind about the career he intended to take up and he entered HMS *Britannia* in 1898.

Cadet Samson was an unusually small boy, no disadvantage in the tween-decks of the old wooden man-of-war, but he was stocky, strong and a respectable boxer. The instruction in knotting and splicing, in gunnery and navigation and in handling a whaler on the lovely River Dart was absorbed without conspicuous effort and as he rose through the grades of "Sixer" and "Niner" – third and fourth term cadet – it seemed a moral certainty that here was the raw material from which admirals were made. Smallness of stature was of no importance in the Navy; indeed it was almost an asset, for Nelson had been a small man and, of the present generation, Sir Henry Keppel, a man even tinier than Samson, was the Admiral most loved and respected for his feats of amazing courage. There was, however, another influence at work. In the same year that Samson entered *Britannia* the novelist Mr. C. J. Cutcliffe Hyne published the first of his Captain Kettle stories. These excellent yarns told of the exciting and near-piratical goings-on of a diminutive Welsh sea captain with a torpedo-shaped beard, a strict Methodist conscience and uncommon skill with what he called a thirty-shilling pistol. The books were deserved best-sellers and many of them were illustrated. It was not Samson's fault that he had early grown a similar beard, in the fashion of Naval officers of a generation then passing, and that the pictures had a likeness to himself. It amused him and, while he did not trade on it, he had no objection to his peers addressing him by the name of this famous figure. It is too late now to find out whether Cutcliffe Hyne drew at all on Drake for his yarns but many of them were placed in the old Spanish Main, though dated in the reign of Queen Victoria, and they told of boardings and cuttings-out of the kind that Sir Francis knew. It gave young Samson something to live up to. He also was pugnacious, a dependable pistol shot and a horseman of more enthusiasm than skill.

Samson climbed the ladder swiftly. In 1903 he was a watchkeeper in HMS *Pomone*, charged with steaming up and down the coast of Somaliland to try and prevent too many modern weapons being smuggled into the country for the use of that elusive man known as the Mad Mullah. In the following year he shipped his second stripe and after a few routine commissions he was back in the Persian Gulf in 1909 as First

Lieutenant of *Philomel*. Prickly heat and the searching of smelly dhows for illicit arms were better value than issuing writs and drafting conveyances and the experience was to prove useful. The Navy, under Fisher and his friends, was changing almost month by month.

In 1901 the Royal Navy moved under the waters with the coming of the "A" Class submarines. Young men of Samson's seniority were torn between the thrusting ideas of youth and the plain suggestions of their elders that to depart from the narrow path and enter "The Trade" was something not far short of treason to the Service. The number of officers needed in the beginning was very small and did not include Charles Samson. Already he was beginning to think about yet a third dimension of sea warfare, one more hazardous and animating even than sailing under the sea. The German Navy was beginning to extend the range of its gun-spotters by the use of airships but no other country was taking them very seriously. Samson was somewhere in the Red Sea carrying out his ordinary "salt horse" officer's duties in *Pomone* when the news came that the proprietors of the Van Cleve Cycle Company, Messrs. Wilbur and Orville Wright, had at last achieved what man had been seeking to do over the centuries. From that moment until his death nearly thirty years later Charles Samson devoted his life to flying with a single-mindedness that few can have equalled.

The new art was slow to catch on in England. France, though denied the prize of being first to make a machine that really flew, was the only country to seize enthusiastically the chances now offered and it was the French Army that first gave hard thought to the uses that could be made of aeroplanes. No Navy was much interested. Gas-bags might have some limited value as spotters provided that the weather stayed fine but there was nothing that a land-based aircraft could contribute to a fleet action. The Royal Navy spoke darkly about "weapons of the weaker power" as it had done when Robert Fulton destroyed a brig with his infernal machine and Mr. Whitehead had demonstrated the torpedo. The First Lord, Mr.

McKenna, specialized in finance and was content to leave the existing order of things undisturbed.

It was in 1911 that winds of change began to blow through the incomparable Coronation summer weather. Mr. Winston Churchill moved up Whitehall from Home Office to Admiralty and Mr. Churchill was the one man not content to live in the past. As a cavalry subaltern he had gone into the fight at Omdurman with a Mauser pistol because it was a better weapon than the sword carried by everybody else. He had read *The Riddle of the Sands* and was alive to the possibility of Germany assembling an invasion fleet behind the Friesian Islands; in case they had such a plan in mind, Mr. Churchill wanted to be able to keep an eye on things and an eye in the air was exactly what he needed. In the same year the War Office, under Mr. Haldane, was coming round to the view that the late CIGS, Sir William Nicholson, had dismissed the consequences of Bleriot's cross-Channel flight a little too summarily and that there was something in aviation after all. The Air Battalion lasted for less than a year and soon gave place to the Naval and Military Wing of the Royal Flying Corps.

The Army had something, though not much, on which to build. British designers and constructors of the stamp of A. V. Roe and Geoffrey de Haviland had persevered in the face of no encouragement, Mr. O'Gorman was at work at Farnborough in the Royal Aircraft Factory and *Punch* found regular entertainment in the slightly grotesque flying cathedral of Colonel (in what service was not clear) Cody, over which much time and money was wasted until its creator crashed it and killed himself. The Navy had also wasted effort building a large airship that never flew, and owned little else, though it did now have a home for its aviators. In 1909 Frank McClean, one of that band of dedicated and forgotten men who gave everything they had to the making of a Flying Service, had bought a tract of suitably flat land near Eastchurch in the Isle of Sheppey, off the North Kent coast, and made a present of it to the Aero Club. Having done this he persuaded the official balloon-makers to the Club (founded in 1901 by Hedges Butler

and C. S. Rolls) to move their workshop from a railway arch at
Battersea to his new field. They were the brothers Eustace and
Oswald Short, joined soon afterwards by their third brother,
Horace. The Shorts had acquired licences to build Wright
machines in England and were expanding into aircraft production using both these and their own designs. McClean bought
four of them, invited Mr. Cockburn, the only British com-
petitor at the Rheims flying meeting, and Mr. Cecil Grace to
come as instructors. When both accepted McClean put the
entire concern at the disposal of the Flying Corps. The First
Lord gratefully accepted it for the Naval Wing and called for
four officers to volunteer for training as pilots. Just over 200
sent in their names and amongst the chosen four was Samson.

They arrived at Eastchurch in October 1911, just as the
most beautiful summer in memory was giving way to a villain-
ous autumn. On the day before instruction was due to begin
Cecil Grace crashed his machine in full view of them all and
was killed. With this encouraging start Cockburn took over all
the flying instruction himself. At once Samson learnt the
advantages of smallness. Cockburn weighed over fourteen
stone; Captain Gregory of the Royal Marines displaced about
the same. On their first flight together the 50 hp Gnome rotary
engine appeared to complain of unfair treatment and their
machine reached its ceiling at about thirty feet. Samson and
Lieutenant Longmore – the Air Marshal of days to come
– fared better and quickly mastered the principles of stick,
throttle and rudder-bar. Their training took place mostly in
gales that made it almost impossible to work up any speed over
the ground, and in one rather spectacular snowstorm. Samson
did not care. He had found out what he was meant to do with
his life and from then on he cared little for other interests.

He had the advantage of being a persuasive talker and often
had a receptive audience. Mr. Churchill has told in his
Thoughts and Adventures how he craftily set aside appropriations
meant for other things in order to furnish the Fleet with the best
aircraft available and much of this was disbursed on Samson's
advice. Before October was out the young Lieutenant had

persuaded the First Lord that Eastchurch must become a regular stone-frigate and a permanent part of the Navy. There was only about a dozen years between them and the two men hit it off perfectly. Samson completed his elementary flying training in six weeks and was at once appointed to the permanent staff. A dozen ratings were sent to train as mechanics, the Admiralty bought the two remaining aircraft from McClean, and Eastchurch became the Royal Navy's Flying School. It was a long way from being a recreational club. Far too many deaths from accidents took place for comfort and the First Lord admits that it required some months to screw up his courage and fly as a passenger. When a Churchill admits to fear there must have been something fearful indeed in the prospect. Once up Mr. Churchill became captivated by the sensation of flight. He demanded that an aeroplane be built with seats for pilot and passenger side by side and in this sociable fashion he spent many hours aloft. With Samson he had long talks about the way to make the new element a useful servant of the old.

Samson was his practical experimenter, along with Lindemann – the famous "Prof" – and one or two others. The matter that exercised the minds of the Naval men can be simply expressed. From Eastchurch to Heligoland is more than 300 miles. No machine in existence or immediate contemplation could travel that far and return. The only answer seemed to be to carry the aeroplane as far as possible by sea and launch it in some fashion from shipboard. The Admiral Superintendent of Chatham Dockyard was told to give Samson a free hand and to supply him with anything he might want. With the ink hardly dry on his Aero Club Pilot's Certificate, Samson drove to Chatham and designed his contraption. After some trial and error he ended up with a platform mounted on a double trackway from which, it was hoped, an aeroplane might be persuaded to stagger into flight. With the First Lord's eager encouragement the platform was transferred bodily to cruiser HMS *Africa* at Sheerness and on a December morning Samson took his seat in the cockpit. The ship was turned into the wind, the little rotary engine warmed itself up, sprinkling castor oil on its attendants; Samson opened the throttle to its full extent – the rotary engine accepts no other position – and the machine lurched forwards and upwards. For a moment it seemed that it would fall ingloriously into the sea but it managed to get itself into the air and was away. Landing again was out of the question; on his return all that Samson could do was pancake under the lee of the ship where an arrangement of air-bags kept him afloat until the aircraft was fished out. So far as it went the flight had been a success but it had taken place in sheltered water and would certainly have failed in a North Sea lop. Even so, it had demonstrated that the thing might be done and when better aircraft with more powerful engines made their appearance it could become a regular evolution. Samson was reasonably well satisfied, but plainly this was not yet the way to get at the German Fleet.

Again he and Mr. Churchill tossed suggestion and counter-suggestion back and forth, taking Horace Short into their counsels. Captain Murray Sueter, the Director of the Admiralty Air Department, and Lord Rayleigh of the National Physical Laboratory also bent their minds to finding an answer. Charles Samson, made up to Commander and put in charge of the Flying School, again was the practical man. From their deliberations came, early in 1912, a craft that was obviously naval; an aeroplane fitted with floats instead of wheels that could both rise from and land upon water. It endured various names until Mr. Churchill ordered that it be called a seaplane. The prototype was finished in the spring of 1912 and taken to Portland for Samson to show what it would do. So well designed and constructed was the machine that Samson flew it for more than 150 hours without the smallest damage. The aircraft carrier was still in the future but the seaplane had become a permanent weapon in the Navy's armoury.

Samson had his Captain Kettle reputation to live up to and this was entirely congenial to him. It was not enough for a seaplane just to look at an enemy ship; it must hit it, and hit it hard. The obvious weapon was some sort of a bomb, but no bomb existed. Even had there been one, what would be the effect on flight of the sudden loss of weight? And what would happen to the seaplane should it cross over the area of the burst? Nobody knew; Samson went to find out. A dummy bomb of 100 lb weight, little less than that of a six-inch shell, was mocked up and fastened below the machine. It took off reluctantly but gained sufficient height and the quick-release gear was worked. Away went the bomb and the pilot, to his surprise, felt not the slightest difference in the handling. One useful lesson learnt. The next was more difficult. As there were no real bombs, a destroyer laid a series of explosive charges on the surface and detonated them from a distance as the seaplane passed over. Below 350 feet the pilot had a shaking but above that height it was imperceptible. Bombing, obviously, was a practicable business.

The next experiment was less encouraging. The main business of the Navy's fliers was still to find the enemy fleet and direct our own squadrons at it, something achievable only by the use of wireless telegraphy. The acknowledged expert in this subject was Lieutenant Fitzmaurice and he and Samson were ordered to find out how the thing should be done. The two men borrowed the wireless equipment from a destroyer, since there was nothing smaller to be had, and somehow managed to install it in a new Short seaplane. On 13 May 1912 they took off from the sea at Yarmouth and set course eastwards to follow the naval manoeuvres. Some twenty miles over the North Sea the engine began to splutter and finally expired. Fitzmaurice managed to get off a message to HMS *Hermes* giving their position but that was the only useful result of the voyage. Short seaplane No. 81 came down in the sea and the crew suffered the indignity of being brought home by a passing German timber ship. A few days later they tried again and managed to transmit a strong signal over a distance of ten miles.

Samson was as happy as the traditional pig in the sunshine. By the following summer he had nearly 100 trained pilots, had made tests not only with seaplane-mounted machine-guns but even with a small cannon, and was a highly respected member of the Air Committee which advised on all flying matters affecting both services. In July 1913, years ahead of its time, he designed and flew a folding aeroplane, taking off this time from HMS *Hermes*, and found it to be "the best and most manageable type". He pioneered night-flying and made his pilots acquire a high degree of proficiency in this most difficult art at a time before the Army had given it serious thought.

On 1 July 1914 the Royal Naval Air Service broke away from the RFC. A fortnight later, at the climax of the Spithead Review, Samson led two full squadrons of seaplanes together with two more of land planes over the assembled Fleet. It was a remarkable achievement in so short a time. As soon as it was over he was sent with an aeroplane squadron to tour the country but they had not got very far when the signal arrived ordering them all back to Eastchurch. With the coming of the war and the despatch of every serviceable Army aeroplane to France the RNAS, he was told, must take on the duty of fighting enemy raiders. There would be no working with the Grand Fleet in any important respect. Had another decision been taken the battle of Jutland might have followed a different pattern.

The Navy had no objection to fighting anybody, but this was not the work for which it had been trained and equipped. In point of strength it had about fifty machines of all kinds, roughly a third of the number owned by the Army; they were, on the whole, better and fitted with the more powerful engines needed to carry their heavier loads but the emphasis had been upon marine aircraft, the seaplanes and the flying-boats that were beginning to emerge from Sopwith's works by Brooklands. With the departure of the RFC, however, only the Navy was left to defend not merely its own ports and installations but the entire east coast of England. It took on the job stoically enough and Samson flew his share of patrols with the rest in the hope of trying out some of their outlandish weapons designed to put fire to the German flying gas-bags. These had appeared over Antwerp in the first days and everybody knew that from their nests at Cuxhaven and Dusseldorf London was within easy reach. None, however, put in an appearance and Samson

became more and more irritated at the lack of useful employ-
ment. He was not kept waiting for long, for Mr. Churchill held
all airships in contempt. Their only virtue was in the height
they could attain, a height that made them invulnerable to any
aeroplane then in service. The sensible thing was to move his
aeroplanes forward to some place on the European mainland
from whence they could hit the Zeppelins as they lay in harbour. This could only be in Belgium and as the right wing of
von Kluck's army swept forward less and less of that brave
kingdom was becoming available. On 1 September, five days
before Maunoury's counter-stroke on the Marne, a minute
went out from the First Lord to Captain Sueter. The largest
possible force of aircraft should be sent at once to Calais or
Dunkirk with the task of searching the country for 70 to 100
miles inland and destroying any Zeppelins that could be
located at rest. Samson was to command with Gerrard as his
2 i/c.

As the German armies moved towards Paris the Belgian
coastal plain became suddenly emptied of large formations of
troops and the German hold was maintained by bodies of
cavalry and by bluff reinforced with terror. Any well-armed
force from either side could, for the moment, go where it
pleased and do anything it wanted. A company of about 250
Royal Marines, mostly reservists and pensioners still dressed
in the old postman-blue uniforms, was all that Britain could
find and they were hurried off to guard the aerodromes as soon
as they could be set up. The BEF was now far away and it was
entirely a Navy affair.

Unknown to the First Lord, Samson's airmen were already
there. Ten pilots, including Samson himself and the Duke of
Westminster's young cousin Lord Edward Grosvenor, had left
Eastchurch on 25 August with an eclectic collection of obsolete
machines. The best land planes that could be found were two
BE biplanes with 70 hp Renault engines, two Sopwith two-
seaters of the kind known to pilots as "Spinning Jennies", one
Bristol and one Short biplane, two Bleriot monoplanes and a
Henri Farman that resembled a stick insect. Their armament

was a ·455 Webley & Scott self-loading pistol apiece – the standard Navy weapon – a rifle carried by Lord Edward and a Lewis gun unaccountably borrowed from a Colonel Lucas of Hobland Hall, Yarmouth. A ninety minute flight from East-church brought them all safely to land on Ostend racecourse. Some Belgian Civil Guards took pot-shots at them as they came in but no harm came of it and on the following day the squadron moved to a better field beyond the town.

Ostend was occupied rather shakily by a Marine Brigade but as it was almost entirely without transport it could do little but wait upon events. General Aston, the commander, was naturally anxious to know what confronted him and invited Samson to take his car and cruise round the district. A second car belonging to Samson's brother Felix, was added to the party, two late Victorian Maxim guns were scraped up from somewhere and a party of four officers and four Marines went off to see what they could find. It turned out to be very little. They drove along almost empty roads to Thourout, where nothing more tangible than a rumour of German cyclists was encountered, and went on to Bruges. There the unhappy Belgians took them for the vedettes of a great army and the Civil Guard quickly resumed the top hats which were their principal article of uniform dress. Nobody had the heart to tell them the truth.

Though his reconnaissance had achieved no useful result, it gave Samson food for thought. If the Germans had nothing more formidable about the place than horses and cyclists, a few armed motor-cars could do damage out of all proportion to their numbers. It would also be immense fun. The next day, however, there came a signal that drove him into fury. The Marines were to go home and so was his squadron. There seemed no reason for this, since Samson had no means of knowing what the Germans were preparing, and he studied the question of how to avoid complying with a disagreeable order without actually disobeying it. It was answered by a stroke of genuine luck. Lord Edward was not yet an experienced pilot. As they came into land at Dunkirk he succeeded in damaging his Bleriot to an extent that made it beyond reason for him to try and take off again. Only Lord Edward could tell whether some calculation entered into it – he was quite capable of giving Fate a little help – and he held his peace. On the same day Mr. Churchill sent his minute to Captain Sueter and the "Dunkirk Circus" became established and legitimated.

For all his piratical appearance Samson was a professional Naval officer before all else and under him Dunkirk took on something of the likeness of a ship. Huts were painted battleship grey and bore labels like "Mess Deck" and "Ward Room". The hours and half-hours were told by bells and men spoke of port and starboard and of going aloft. "Never once," he wrote to Sir Walter Raleigh the historian of the flying services, "were we let down by our men and . . . they worked like slaves. It is an absolute fact that during these periods I never had to deal with a single disciplinary offence. They were the very pick of the Royal Naval Air Service." The buccaneering aspect of the business showed itself most in the appearance of the fliers. As no special kit had been issued each wore what he pleased and some weird coats and mufflers appeared above the leather sea-boots that were the only standard wear. A school of thought insisted that it was wise to fill these with brandy to keep out the cold but the habit never really caught on. There was better use for it.

All this work took time and Samson was impatient to hit the Germans as soon as he could. If he could not attack their ships then troops on the ground must serve for the time being. While the aerodrome was being prepared and two more squadrons fitted in he decided that as he had enjoyed his earlier foray he would see what could be done about clearing the countryside with armed motor-cars. The Director of the Air Division and the First Lord were entirely in sympathy with him and ordered the formation of an armoured car force. Mr. Churchill, who had been much taken by the reported exploits of a single Belgian machine, gave the matter his personal attention and in a very short time no less than seven or eight squadrons were called into being, based on the purchase of all the Rolls-Royce cars that were available and rapidly improvised armoured protection.' The best was always good enough for the Royal Navy. By mid-September the garrison had grown by a Marine Brigade, a regiment of Yeomanry cavalry and "fifty motor omnibuses taken from the London streets". The Channel ports could no longer be taken at a run and Samson's guerrilleros would not need to stay too near home. He approached the local French commander, General Bidon (a name that can be translated as "petrol can") and obtained a letter giving him licence to do as he pleased on French soil.

Rising from the flat Flanders plain is a steep hill upon which stands the ancient town of Cassel. A little to the south lies the Chateau de la Motte, a building as old as recorded history and grimly held throughout the war by its splendid chatelaine. Though parties of German soldiers were roaming all round the countryside Mme. la Baronne de la Grange did not deign to be driven out, holding her duty to her tenantry as a sacred trust. On a fine September morning a strange aeroplane, not French, flew over the chateau and the Baroness took her basset hound to find out what was going on. "At that moment two armoured cars stopped in the courtyard. My first impression was that they were Germans and my heart stood still." Samson introduced himself and, having found to his relief that the lady spoke English, invited her to come with him and direct the aeroplane to some suitable landing place. The Baroness seated herself in one car, her neighbour the Count de Moras entered the other and she directed them to a meadow near Morbecques where the Russians had camped in 1814, and where now, under Samson's instructions, she learned how to beckon the lost machine down. That done, the Baroness went with him to the village to arrange about billets. While they were so employed a car appeared in a cloud of dust coming from the direction of Hazebrouck; Samson shoved her quickly under cover, saying that the Germans often arrived like that and "peppered everything". It turned out to be nothing more lethal than the Sub-Prefect of Hazebrouck out on his lawful occasions. Samson lunched at the Chateau on "macaroni, tongue and jam with a bottle of old Burgundy emptied to the toast of the Entente Cordiale" and was lectured on the necessity of holding Cassel. Whilst they were thus engaged the aeroplane landed in the meadow without help from either of them.

Samson knew Cassel quite well. A few days previously he told her, he had been tipped off by telephone that six German officers in a staff car were heading in its direction from Bailleul. It seemed a pity to neglect the chance of an ambush on the steep winding hill that leads into the little town but Cassel was unprotected and a terrible vengeance might be taken on the pretence of *franc-tireur* activity. With two cars, one carrying the Maxim, Samson had lain up for his victims by the roadside. Somebody – it would not have been Samson – lost his head at the sight of them coming and had opened up at 500 yards. The car turned and Samson made suitable observations to his gunner. They had waited for a couple of hours; an elderly gentleman with a pistol of antique pattern had came to join them, explaining that he was a retired Captain of Gendarmes, had raised a force of ten of his old comrades and would like to take a hand. The Germans, however, had not come back. Next day the cars had something more spectacular to do, for General Bidon telephoned excitedly to say that the Germans were marching out of Lille – the battle of the Marne was about to open – and he wanted to scoop up the transport they would surely have left behind. Would Samson please come and escort his small force of infantry? He would gladly lend him two St. Etienne machine-guns and four men to work them. On the morning of 6 September, the day the tide turned, four cars set off for Lille escorted in turn by a single aeroplane. Not a German was to be seen; the cars drove happily into the Place d'Armes and lined up in front of the Prefecture surrounded by a vast crowd. Samson posted sentries and went inside to see the Prefect, observing with pleasure as he went that "our sentries stood like Guardsmen and even when beautiful French girls came on the scene and sponged their faces and brushed the dust off their clothes, they stood like lumps of granite". As the legend round the clock at Osborne used to proclaim, "There is nothing the Navy cannot do."

The Prefect had been badly roughed-up by a German officer who had threatened to hang him from his balcony; he gave the miscreant's name to the sailor who made a note of it, just in case. Then the Prefect told what little news he had. Apparently the one burst from the Maxim outside Cassel had wounded two of the officers in the car and had given the impression that a strong English force was about the place. There were about fifty French wounded, together with a few British, in Lille. If the Commander cared to occupy the town he could have them, otherwise the Germans would hold the Prefect guilty of helping the Allies. On a sheet of paper Samson obligingly if inaccurately wrote as follows: "To the authorities of the City of Lille. I have this day occupied Lille with an armed English and French force. C. R. Samson, Commander RN, Officer in Command of English Force at Dunkirk." This was pure Captain Kettle, who had done something of the same kind more than once though on a lower level. The Germans had, seemingly, taken all their transport with them and by late afternoon, as "there was no chance of any French troops being sent to Lille, I reluctantly decided that I ought to return to Dunkirk. We had an ovation on our return journey through the streets, and our cars were full of flowers, chocolate, cigarettes, etc.; the dense crowds cheered themselves hoarse and one felt rather as I imagined a Roman General used to feel on being given a Triumph. The only mishap was when an excitable individual threw a bottle of beer at me which smashed the screen and gave me a severe blow in the face; I fancy he must have had German sympathies."

Samson was gaining a local reputation beyond anything he had yet earned. A few days after the Lille trip he went to Armentieres where another civilian in a motor-car waylaid him. He knew a place, he said, where there were two or three thousand Germans with two batteries of artillery just waiting for Samson to come and kill them. The Commander, not sure whether to take this at its face value, said mildly that this seemed rather long odds for four Englishmen with an old and unreliable Maxim. "He was very crestfallen, and said 'But I will come too'." The odds still seemed too long.

It was not all a motoring holiday in late summer weather. The Marne had left large bands of German stragglers and deserters lurking about the woods and preying on the local people. They were well armed and could be dangerous. As more cars came in and the Forges et Chantiers de France, the Dunkirk shipbuilders, found boiler-plate and armoured them in some fashion, many had to be given the job of rounding these up. German cavalry still roamed about far from the main battle and were just the sort of targets an armoured car wanted. Samson drove further and further afield. On 13 September, just outside Doullens on the Albert road, some of the cars almost literally ran into a body of them. Lacking proper machine-gun mountings, they left the cars and opened up with rifle fire. "We hit five of them. Three were killed and one was picked up severely wounded. We took him to a hospital in Doullens where he died without recovering consciousness." The unfortunate man, who looked half-starved, "had a little child's atlas with a map of France about three inches square with only the names of half a dozen towns on it".

Dunkirk was getting too small and too remote for these extended enterprises and on 19 September Samson, with the permission of the Baroness, took over the meadow at Morbecque for an advanced base. As the cars were slow to arrive from England he acquired bicycles – bicycle-making was Albert's main industry – and mounted his surplus Marines on them under the guidance of the local Boy Scouts. The purpose behind it all was to be ready to join with the French in a serious attack on the German lines of communication behind Lille and Valenciennes; as the French could muster only a brigade of Territorials, men even older than Samson's Marine pensioners, and a squadron of "goums" – Algerian cavalry – supported by a battery of 75s they would need all the help they could get. They had their little battle at Orchies on 22 September. Samson obviously set some store by it as he put in his *Who's Who*

entry for years that he had "commanded a French Territorial
Brigade at the battle of Orchies". This was true, and details are
scrappy but it does seem that they were attacked by two
German battalions; the old gentlemen ran away and were
shepherded back to Douai by the cars which discouraged all
attempts by the Germans to exploit their success. The "Race to
the Sea" had begun and Samson, all unwitting, was driving
towards the advancing German armies. On the day after
Orchies he was asked to investigate the village of Cantin, about
three miles south of Douai, and set off in a Talbot car with two
other officers. The sight of large enemy forces marching north
sent them packing back to Douai, soon to be surrounded, and
this time they were in a serious scrape. On the afternoon of 1
October the end came. By that time the Germans had got into
the town and were firing at the Hotel de Ville from the house-
tops. "A shouting mob of cyclists and infantry rushed into the
courtyard shouting that we were surrounded and the Germans
had taken the Pont d'Esquerchin. I went to General Plantey
and said that the only thing to do was to recapture the bridge
and drive the Germans away from that sector. He agreed and
said that if I would lead the way with my cars he would follow
with what of the troops he could get to fight. There was no
doubt that if we did not do something a wholesale surrender
was certain. I strongly objected to being mixed up in that. I felt
certain that if only we could start a fight the morale would
improve and that we would have every chance of extricating
the whole force from its predicament." He was over-optimistic.
The two cars forced their way through the crowd until they
came in sight of the bridge, where Samson halted in order to get
some of the several hundred infantry milling about aimlessly to
come and join him. All the curses of an experienced Naval
officer were wasted. Apart from one stout fellow who jumped
on to the last car, every man refused to come. Samson, in a
tearing rage, rushed for the bridge, got his Marines out into the
road and put them to firing bursts from their three machine-
guns into the enemy across the canal and down both the
transverse roads. Covered by their fire he rushed the bridge

alone, followed by a single Marine, and emptied the magazine of his pistol into some Germans gathered on the far bank. "We were so excited that I am afraid our fire was very wild, but it made up for lack of accuracy by its volume, our three machine-guns firing like mad. We kept up this game for about five minutes, when I saw the Germans clearing off in all directions. I gave the 'Cease Fire' and ordered all on board the cars. I then led the cars at full speed along the Henin – Lietard road." Something like a mile further on a road came in from the left leading to Beaumont. Here they came under heavy fire and Samson got his men under cover in some ruined cottages. After some fifteen minutes German guns began to search the area and the cottages disappeared in a haze of pink dust. There was nothing for it but to get out quickly and Samson led the cars in a dash down the Esquerchin road, to the left and so far unblocked. They made about a mile before he stopped to take stock. All the cars were patterned with bullet holes, one had a shot through the radiator, eight men were wounded, ammunition was down to a total of 200 rounds and they were nearly out of petrol. Samson, reasonably enough, felt honour to be satisfied and made for the safety of Beaumont, where French cavalry had been reported. Only later did he learn that their stand at the road junction had distracted the Germans for long enough to allow General Plantey to bring 2,500 of his men across the bridge and away without a shot being fired at them. The little band made its way back to Morbecques to which place General Plantey sent a message that had it not been for the English cars he could not have extricated his force. General Paris, who had taken over the Marine Brigade from General Aston, signalled to the Admiralty that "Commander Samson and all ranks appear to have behaved very gallantly and I consider his action was perfectly correct."

Now it was to be the turn of Antwerp. A large German force, not engaged in the opening battles, was closing in equipped with demolition machinery in the shape of the Skoda mortars that had smashed Liege and Namur. The only possible reinforcement from England, a very scratch Naval division, was

put into the City to try and keep it from falling as the other
fortresses had done. The task of the RNAS was to move some
aircraft into Antwerp while the opportunity remained and to
strike the Zeppelin sheds at Dusseldorf.

Samson posted to Antwerp as fast as he could go but his part
in the battle was relatively unimportant. On 22 September two
very brave men had flown over both Dusseldorf and Cologne
but luck had been against them; their bombs either missed or
failed to explode and the damage done was trifling. On 8
October, as the crowds were pouring out of Antwerp to the
west under a pall of blazing oil tanks, a last attempt was made.
Flight-Lieutenant Marix dropped his bombs over the Dusseldorf sheds from 600 feet, saw the flames that could only mean a
Zeppelin burning, was shot down by ground fire and finished
the last twenty miles of his journey on a bicycle. Commander
Spenser Grey reached Cologne but was denied the same satisfaction; as mist hid the target from him, he dropped his load on
the railway station and came safely back to Antwerp. The
Germans could now see that the arm of the Royal Navy was a
long one.

Sir Henry Rawlinson, whose IV Corps never reached Antwerp but saved Ypres and the Channel Ports, was the soldier
Samson most admired. "I never saw him downhearted once,
even in the worst periods at Ypres. I never left his presence
without feeling that we were bound to win." Such language,
used of soldiers, does not come naturally to a sailor and is
worth recording.

Very soon now the German army was moving west along the
sea coast, harrying what was left of the unhappy Belgians
behind the Yser. Plugs were pulled out and the waters slowly
rose between them, denying use to either side of the land
immediately fronting the sea. The Germans, always sensitive
to the idea of a sea-landing in their rear, began to fortify the
coast. The RNAS from Dunkirk devoted itself to frustrating
their purpose.

It was mainly the business of the old Navy, part of it a very
old Navy indeed. The right wing of the German Army could

not be permitted to build itself up in strength preparatory to an attack in the direction of the Channel ports, nor could the German Navy be given uninterrupted use of its fine new harbours at Ostend and Zeebrugge. Within a day or two of its arrival there the First Lord had assembled an odd-looking flotilla designed to deny the new tenants their quiet enjoyment. Old battleships that could creep over the sandbanks with inches to spare and whose guns could use up stocks of obsolete shells, new monitors lately building for neutral countries and taken over from them together with some veteran gunboats that had been a little-regarded part of the old Queen's Navy set out to pound the Belgian littoral. As few of them could command any view over the sand dunes their fire must be blind unless eyes could be found. Samson and his squadrons provided them. Fewer motoring adventures for them now; the war of movement was finished for four years and they could go back to the interrupted task of naval co-operation.

Very early on Samson visited Nieuport, the last place on the Belgian coast in the hands of Belgian troops. His trip there was of no great importance in itself but in the process he came by one who was to be his constant companion for the rest of the war; a small white dog, described by his new owner to Compton Mackenzie as "the last inhabitant." The little animal soon became a kind of squadron mascot and was well known to everybody in the Service.

In mid-October the shipyard that had armoured the cars was taken over and became a seaplane base. With this reinforcement Naval aircraft set out to deal with the enemy-held ports while the land-based machines spotted for ships' guns and kept the air clear of opposition. The locks and basins at Ostend and Zeebrugge might have been designed, in conjunction with the canal system linking them to Bruges, for operations by marauding light craft. The flat Belgian fields were equally perfect for the establishment of Zeppelin bases within easy range of the most important targets in England. Samson and his men bombed by night and bombed by day, gradually increasing their skill and equipment. Their reward was largely negative, counted in the number of things the enemy could not do rather than by anything spectacular. It was every bit as useful and one can only guess at what England was spared by their efforts.

Somewhere about this time Commander E. R. G. R. Evans, not yet "Evans of the Broke", visited Dunkirk to discuss air-spotting on behalf of his chief, Admiral Hood. "Those chaps were never idle," he recalled, "and if the weather were unfit for flying and there was nothing they could invent better to annoy the enemy, one, who shall be nameless, would finish his glass of port and say 'Come on, you fellows, let's go and shoot Uhlans', and away would roll the great drab-coloured motor-car. It went everywhere, and seldom returned without a German helmet or two which had scarcely cooled off the warmth derived from the late lamented owner."

Negative successes were not enough for Samson and his masters. One of the strangest characters to emerge from the war was Mr. Noel Pemberton-Billing. He was born rich, the son of a Birmingham ironmaster, and being free from the necessity of earning a living he set out to enjoy himself. At the age of 19 he volunteered for South Africa and saw some service there; on his return he became captivated by the idea of flying. In 1908 he founded and edited a magazine called *Aerocraft* and it is said that he learned to fly within a period of twenty-four hours in order to win a bet. He was one of the first batch of RNAS Lieutenants to be commissioned but he did not go to Dunkirk with the original "Circus". Instead, he had been privily sent to Switzerland to find out all he could about the Zeppelin works at Friedrichshaven on Lake Constance. This was the most important target of all, the place where the things were made, and Pemberton-Billing advised that an attack from the air, with all the advantages of surprise, would be a practicable proposition. A squadron of four naval aircraft had been got together at Manchester for the purpose; two of the pilots were original Eastchurch men who had gone out with Samson, Lieutenants Briggs and Sippé. By arrangement with the French, the four Avro machines were taken piecemeal by road to Belfort, whence a flight of 125 miles over the Black Forest would bring them on to the sheds they were seeking. Soon after breakfast on 21 November the aircraft began to take off at five-minute intervals each carrying four 20 lb bombs. One failed to leave the ground but the other three all reached Friedrichshaven together after a flight of some ninety minutes. Sippé dropped three bombs squarely on target, the fourth jamming in the release gear, and saw great sheets of flame leap into the sky. Briggs and Babington pretty certainly scored hits, for a Swiss engineer who saw it all counted nine explosions within 700 square yards. Ground fire was very heavy and Briggs was brought down, his machine shot through the petrol tank. The other two returned unhurt, though Babington ran out of petrol and force-landed in a field. He arrived back at Belfort to be told by Pemberton-Billing that his Swiss agent had already reported the success of the raid. It was not a small thing to have flown these tiny, under-powered and not over-reliable aircraft to the limit of their endurance across forest and mountain into a place that must inevitably be well defended. Nothing like it had been done before and the DSOs were well earned. Briggs, in hospital, was treated by the German officers with admiration and kindness, for all air services took pride in their civilized behaviour.

It was the culminating point in Pemberton-Billing's career. In 1916 he left the Service and went into Parliament with the object of trying to force the government to provide better aircraft and engines, declaiming loudly about the "murder" of young flying officers. Though there was much in what he said it contributed nothing to the knowledge already possessed by the authorities, nor did it do anything for morale. Later on he came to the conclusion that the war effort was being sabotaged by a homosexual coven in the highest places and his notorious *Black Book* was the subject of much argument. He was treated with contempt and disgust, being in July 1918 ejected from the Commons; one can only hope he deserved it.

The coming of winter inevitably cut down all flying, but the Navy was out in all but the foulest weather, beating up gun positions, port installations, oil tanks and ships. On Christmas Eve 1914, as Commodores Tyrwhitt and Keyes steamed into Heligoland Bight with the light cruisers and destroyers of Harwich Force, the author of *The Riddle of the Sands* looked down from the observer's cockpit of Seaplane No. 136 on the scenes of drama and excitement of a dozen years before. Lieutenant Erskine Childers RNVR wrote in his notebook of battleships and cruisers in Schillig Roads, of ships in the Weser estuary and of destroyers lying off Wangeroog. No other man had the encyclopaedic knowledge of that low-tide desert. On the same day a German aeroplane dropped its bomb in the garden of Mr. Terson, a burgess of Dover.

Samson and his men patrolled and spotted and bombed, keeping the left of the line busy, as 1914 passed into 1915. He was on the crest of the wave; the Legion of Honour and Croix de Guerre had come to him from the French for the affair at Douai, to be followed by the DSO, a decoration valued by both flying services where it testified to more than the glorified service stripe which was common in the Army. Above all, his doings had caught the fancy of Mr. Churchill. In the First Lord's eyes Samson was Naval Aviation and Naval Aviation was Samson. It was a little hard on some other officers, but there it was.

When the Mediterranean Expeditionary Force was being scraped together for the assault on the Dardanelles there was only one name that came to mind in Whitehall to run the flying side of it. When the sea bombardment of the outer forts took place in the first days of March three seaplanes had been there to spot for the guns. In Mr. Churchill's words: "The first machine sent up crashed owing to the propeller bursting at 3,000 feet. The second machine was forced to descend after being hit six times by rifle bullets and the pilot wounded. The third machine gave one correction only." The snarled contempt of that famous voice comes through the bald prose. He needed better than this and ordered up the man he knew. Samson was not pleased, for he was busily engaged where he was, but he had no choice and accepted the command.

In the last days of March 1915, after the Navy had turned back from the Straits, No. 3 Squadron RNAS arrived at Tenedos; it mustered eleven pilots, including Samson, three observers, two technical officers, a doctor and 100 men. Their aircraft had been left at Dunkirk and in exchange they had been issued with what seemed the makings of a museum. There were eighteen aeroplanes in all, eleven of them veteran Farmans of both Henri and Maurice varieties; another was the original BE2c that Samson had used for experiments at Eastchurch. None was reliable, all were slow and capable of reaching only modest heights even with minimal loads. Lieutenant Butler happened to own a small Goertz folding camera; this, to which was later added a slightly better one borrowed from an obliging French officer, became the squadron's photographic equipment. There were a few bombs in store but no other weapons. Samson's Standing Orders demanded that "Pilots always be armed with a revolver or pistol; to carry binoculars; some safety device, either waistcoat, patent lifebelt or petrol can." Poor tools were no excuse for inactivity. "If an enemy aeroplane is sighted, attack it, reporting you are doing so if spotting," ending with a warning against stunt flying. "This is not wanted in war, and is not conduct required of an officer."

The Admiral, Sir John de Robeck, gave the aeroplanes the immediate neighbourbood of the Straits as their charge, to be watched and photographed regularly while his seaplanes went further afield. Cape Helles was about eighteen miles away and the cove which would soon be known as Anzac something over thirty; quite long distances for aircraft little, if any, better than the original Bleriot. In the days before 25 April the veterans rumbled into the air, spitting sand from their rotary engines, and flew uncertainly over the Turkish lines around the beaches, mapping as best they could, spotting for the naval guns within the limits of their ability and taking crude photographs of what they saw. The wireless worked one way only and signals were acknowledged by ships' searchlights, but it was better than nothing at all. Fortunately the Turks were no better off in the matter of aircraft.

Samson was under no illusions about the dreadful ordeal waiting for the infantry. On the day of the landing, as *River Clyde*'s forefoot crunched into the sand, he was overhead. "It was rotten," he wrote, "seeing the soldiers get hell at the landing places. Knowing the defences I did not believe they would be able to get ashore." As he came in low over Sedd-el-Bahr in a flat calm "the blue sea was absolutely red with blood for a distance of 50 yards from the shore, a horrible sight to see". A series of waves not likely in such weather he recognized as being lines of enemy machine-gun bullets ploughing up the water. There was nothing he could do beyond reporting regularly to Sir Ian Hamilton, with whom he was in close confidence. A single squadron of decent aircraft with machine-guns would have more than earned their pay; Samson did not waste time on this occasion with his pistol. It was too serious for gestures.

He had a better opportunity on 18 May. Marix, of Zeppelin fame, had noticed unusual activity in the port of Ak Bashi Liman, which suggested the arrival of a fresh Turkish division to reinforce the ones that were trying to eject the Anzacs from their stronghold. The squadron owned an experimental Breguet, a machine designed for bombing but with an engine so untrustworthy that it had been used but once. It was the only aircraft capable of the task the two men had in mind and mechanics were set to work on it. Samson again blessed his lack of weight, for it allowed a 100 lb bomb to be carried in addition to fourteen of the usual twenty-pounders. Marix piloted with Samson in the observer's seat and on a sunny afternoon the Breguet arrived over the docks, where the activity was plain to see. The Turks regarded the place as safe and took no precautions; the big bomb followed by a shower of small ones landed in the harbour area killing and wounding more than fifty men and creating a satisfactory panic amongst the rest. The report brought back to General Birdwood gave the Australians and New Zealanders fair warning of the coming attack and they dealt with it so thoroughly that an armistice had to be arranged for the burial of the Turkish dead.

Compton Mackenzie, as a temporary Marine officer on Sir Ian Hamilton's staff, saw the negotiations for this being carried on. Later on he decided to visit an old friend with whom he had been up at Magdalen, Bill Samson, the Commander's elder brother who had broken an ankle when thrown out of his aeroplane off Mytilene. Charles Samson invited him to stay for a meal but as he seemed intent on some ploy Mackenzie demurred. Samson replied casually: "Oh, I shall be back in twenty minutes, I'm only going to drop this bomb on Yeni Keui." "Off he went with one of those hundred-pounders like an Indian club to leave his mark on the southern side of the Straits." They did, however, dine together on another occasion. "The men working inside the hangars had lighted their lamps, and the great emerald tents were glowing like the luminous eyes of giant cats . . . On the level ground which ran down before us to the beach two French aeroplanes were quivering like newly emerged moths before they made a short trial flight; and a little white dog, looking so very little in all that grandeur of colour and line and atmosphere, was growling excitably to himself as he worried a ball of cotton wool." Just such a sight might Drake have seen any evening at Port Pheasant, save for the aeroplanes. Mackenzie had got it into his head that Samson was in the habit of bombing Constantinople and asked whether he might accompany him on the next trip. "I cannot pretend that I was much disappointed when he refused."

The improvisation that marked everything to do with the Gallipoli campaign was nowhere plainer to see than in the air service. "There was not even a good camera and the very observers were mostly untrained midshipmen chosen like jockeys or coxes for their lack of weight. So it was not surprising to find a Mess in which one felt the absence of any tradition except a dauntless gallantry, and the consciousness of sudden death at the elbow. A small hot marquee. Two dozen men in various oddments of uniform or shirt-sleeves sitting along a trestle table, eating bread and jam and drinking large cups of very much sweetened tea. Plenty of flies, but not as many as elsewhere, not more than you would find in a village grocer's towards the end of a hot August, and perhaps the comparison to a village grocer's is suggested by my recollection of the smell of the dry packing cases on which we sat. At the head of the table Samson himself, a thick-set man with a trim brown beard. The conversation is almost entirely about aeroplane parts, or so it seems to me as I look back 14 years later, aeroplane parts and a few schoolboy jokes." Samson, in or out of the Mess, was an unmistakable figure, for the sun had made him take to wearing a Wolseley helmet. This is an efficient form of headdress for its purpose but it is large and tends to extinguish the wearer should he be small; very small men take on the air of ambulant mushrooms and Samson was no exception.

At the end of May the first German submarines began to put in an appearance and Samson interested himself in them. When one of his pilots told him that he had seen a suspicious object off Rabbit Island Samson had a 100 lb bomb lashed under the BE and went out to look for it. The pilot had not erred; it was Commander Hersing's U21. Samson dived on the submerged shape and let go his bomb which exploded on the surface of the water. Hersing sold him a dummy by swimming underneath the French battleship *Henri IV*. Samson, much chagrined, went home; later in the day he was up again and saw the submarine quietly making her way home on the surface off Ak Bashi Liman. He had no bomb but this time a gesture was irresistible. Samson dropped to a few feet above the water and treated her to a magazine from his pistol. It was not satisfying, for a torpedo-carrying aircraft would have found her an easy target. In his *World Crisis* Mr. Churchill speaks of the failure to develop such machines as "one of the great crimes of the war" and Samson would have agreed with him. A few months later Commander Edmonds released a torpedo from a Short seaplane and hit a small Turkish steamer, but it was an isolated piece of virtuosity.

In October Bulgaria came into the war and it was highly desirable to cut the railway joining that country with Turkey. The most promising point was the bridge over the river

Maritza, south of Kuleli Burgas and just within extreme aircraft range. The task was given to Samson in an aeroplane and Commander Edmonds in a Short seaplane. The aerodrome had been moved from Tenedos to Imbros, from which Samson was to start on a round trip of just under 200 miles. Edmonds was to travel in the seaplane carrier *Ben-my-Chree* as far as Enos and would have to fly about eighty miles less. The only possible aeroplane was a Maurice Farman pusher fitted with extra petrol tanks; with two 112 lb bombs and even with the lightweight Samson and his observer it was loaded to more than its capacity. Add to this that sixty miles of the journey would be over the sea and some idea of the danger can be obtained. The museum-piece aeroplane reached the target and Samson let go his bombs at 800 feet. Either by extreme good judgment, extreme good luck or a combination of both he missed the target by only five yards, damaging one of the piers enough to stop traffic for a couple of days. The seaplane missed the bridge but tore up some of the permanent way. With the primitive tools available it was not a bad try by either of them. As soon as it became plain that the thing might be done the railway became a regular target for small formations of bombers and over it, eleven days after Samson's visit, Commander Bell Davis won his Victoria Cross.

These isolated episodes are, of course, only some of the more spectacular feats recorded to Samson's credit and, baldly stated, they may suggest that he was a man given to hogging the limelight. This would be to do him great injustice. His view of the matter was simple and correct. These were operations of a kind never before attempted and for which no guidance could be found. It was therefore only fitting that the senior officer present should be the first to take them on, especially when he was the most experienced pilot. Samson was surrounded by a fine body of fliers all of whom were given more than enough work to do and he took his share of the humdrum business of reconnoitring over the enemy lines, directing fire from the ships' guns and photographing whatever could be photographed. For a time he had an advanced airstrip on Cape

Helles itself from which it was his custom to take off early in the morning, wave his way over the British positions and cheer up the infantry a little by showing that they were not entirely friendless. When the Turkish gunners got the range of the strip he amused himself by planting a dummy aeroplane on it and watching them waste some 500 shells over its destruction. When better aircraft began to come in he took over a Nieuport with a Lewis gun and with it made himself a considerable nuisance to the Turks. In the course of one of these little expeditions he came close to changing the future history of Europe.

It happened in this fashion. On 18 September Samson was flying round the Anzac position meditating mischief when he spied a big staff car containing three passengers, one of whom appeared to be a General. He naturally chased it and dropped one of his small bombs which hit the road immediately behind. The occupants got out and dived for cover. By the time Samson had made his turn and was coming in for a second run the car was under way again and he dropped his other bomb. This was nearer, breaking the windscreen and wounding the driver, but it did not disable the vehicle. As Samson's Lewis gun could only fire on an upward angle there was no more damage he could do. This was fortunate for Turkey, as the General was Mustafa Kemal Pasha, returning home on sick leave.

The campaign was, for Samson, a series of small successes but larger frustrations. He had watched helplessly as the first landings were decimated; he was despatched to examine, photograph and report upon the suitability of Suvla Bay for a new thrust and produced hard evidence that the Turks were in no great strength there. Once troops had been landed they could and must move quickly across the plain into the foothills, brushing aside such small opposition as they found. Sir Ian Hamilton thought the same. Lieutenant-General Sir Frederick Stopford did not. His men landed and had an extended picnic while holes were dug to accommodate the guns when they should arrive. Once again the Turks were given comfortable time in which to make ready and the operation was entirely wasted. This is not the place to examine whether or not, under other leaders, it might have come off and changed the entire campaign and the war.

When the evacuation came it pointed the fact that the friendship of Mr. Churchill was no longer a thing to be sought. Sir Ian Hamilton was never employed again and, on a lower level, Samson was relegated to the side-lines. In the ten months since he had left Dunkirk new names had been made and he was not invited to return.

All the same, work of a kind was found for him, work of a kind that Drake would have loved. A number of ships had been got together for the flying side of the Dardanelles campaign, ships ranging from the fast Isle of Man ferry *Ben-my-Chree*, used as a seaplane tender, to the kite-balloon ship *Manica* which in civil life had carried dung up and down the Manchester Ship Canal. Some use had to be found for them. A squadron of sorts was put together, *Ben-my-Chree*, the ex-German steamer *Raben-fels* re-named *Raven II*, and the old ferry-steamer *Empress*. Distributed between them was a collection of seaplanes and flying-boats. Samson was given command and ordered to base himself on Port Said with the object of keeping up a surveillance of the entire coast line from Bardia, eastwards to Egypt, up the coast of Palestine, Syria and Asia Minor with an occasional excursion as far as Aden. He took over in February 1916, just in time to be the first pilot over the Western Desert, watching the goings-on of the Senussi around Bardia and Sollum. A month later he took *Raven* with six seaplanes to Aden, then invested by the Turks, and sallied out with Edmonds to bomb their camps. During their time on Tenedos they had experimented with 25-gallon petrol drums as an adjunct to the ordinary bomb and these were dropped now upon the Turkish gun positions with satisfactory results. In June, just as great fleets were grappling off Jutland and both Jellicoe and Beatty would have bartered their souls for a decent spotter-plane force, Samson was off Perim, bombing Turkish camps in the Lahej delta. Then he was back up the Red Sea again, this time to spot for the monitor M21 which was shelling the retreating Turks after their defeat at Romani. The first of the many bombs to fall in Sinai came from Samson's seaplanes as they set about Turkish dumps and stores gathered there for the invasion of Egypt. It would be agreeable to write of Samson reconnoitring Gaza; the squadron did indeed bomb the town but not until October 1917, by which time he was elsewhere.

Alexandretta, the "armpit of the Turkish Empire", was a place well deserving of attention. It received frequent visits from the seaplanes, though they caused more consternation than damage; Adana, in Anatolia, had the misfortune to be near the long girder bridges carrying railway lines over the rivers Jeihan and Seihan and these too received regular attention. Once again the damage was slight for these important places were well defended and it would be many years before the art of bombing had developed enough to be able to wreck such from heights beyond gun range. Samson did not have it all his own way. On a day in January 1917 *Ben-my-Chree* took up a position behind the island of Kastelorizo off the Syrian coast. This time the Turks were expecting her, with a new battery ready and waiting. A few shells quickly sent her to the bottom in shallow water and Samson was lucky to get his men off without loss. *Empress* and *Raven,* heavily overloaded, withdrew from the scene. At Port Said further orders were waiting that would finally take Samson away from the waters of the Levant.

By the beginning of 1917 the Navy had swept up nearly all the German surface raiders. *Wolf,* however, remained elusive. With an armament equal to anything less than a light cruiser and carrying her own seaplane to enlarge her vision *Wolf* could be not merely a nuisance but a danger. She was known to be in the Indian Ocean but that exhausted the Admiralty's knowledge of her lurking place. Samson was to take one ship, such seaplanes as could be carried, find *Wolf* and destroy her. He chose *Raven* as being the faster and set off in company with an elderly French cruiser down the Red Sea once more and across to Bombay for coal. Thus replenished they could, with good fortune, scour the ocean and find their enemy. *Raven* carried only two small guns; if they should meet in the absence of the Frenchman, who was a very slow steamer, it would have to be the seaplanes that must do the fighting. No aircraft had yet fought it out with a warship but the prospect was a stimulating one.

They began by combing the archipelagoes of the Laccadives and Maldive Islands, pirate country of old and capable of hiding a pack of *Wolves*. From high above the ocean Samson looked down; tropical islands by the score, coral and palm trees set in an unimaginable blueness broken only by the fins of sharks or a sudden explosion of flying-fish mocked him. No more than the odd dhow was to be seen, never so much as a whiff of smoke. Day after day the seaplanes and the little Sopwith flying-boat took off, from a lagoon when they could but over the rollers of an Indian Ocean swell when there was no alternative. Great distances were flown over this vast oceanic wilderness, bringing in nothing but negative information. Back to Colombo for coal and off they went again, this time to look at the South Male and Are Atolls. Colombo remembered Captain von Muller and the *Emden* and was understandably nervous.

This last sweep produced an adventure that was straight out of Captain Kettle though it was Mr Kipling who made a story out of it under the name of *A Flight of Fact*. Sub-Lieutenant Smith and Lieutenant Meade took off one morning as usual for a routine search in their Short seaplane. In the course of their flight a tropical rainstorm began to inundate them, blackening the sky and forcing the aircraft down by sheer weight of water. Meade managed to find a spot under cover of an islet but underestimated the clinging power of coral and the machine stuck fast. After heroic efforts they forced it clear and got it airborne, only to have to land again for lack of petrol. This time they were compelled to beachcomb, living on coconuts brought down by fire from their Lewis gun, until eventually they were brought home to Colombo in a Maldivian felucca. Samson, who had written them off as lost, was already there to greet them and made arrangements for the salvage of the aircraft.

It may have been that Mr Churchill was back in the Cabinet and learned how the talents of one of the best of the Navy's flying officers was being wasted, looking for a ship already far away; it may have been simply a routine posting. Whatever it was, while *Raven* was swinging round her mooring in Colombo harbour orders came aboard for Samson to return home at once by mail steamer. It was time for him to come back to the real war and by this he was well pleased.

It was nearing autumn 1917 when Charles Samson came home, the first time apart from some fleeting visits since the war had begun. On this occasion he took a little time off to marry before moving on to his next assignment. When he had left Dunkirk the total strength of the RNAS had been about 600: it was now something in the order of 45,000 and a very different proposition. Naval air stations, equipped with new and good machines, now ringed the island though still most of its strength was put out around the North Sea. Here the sovereign weapon was the flying-boat and its entrepreneur was Commander Porte. He had left the Navy in consequence of a flying injury before the war and had settled in the United States where he worked with Mr. Glenn Curtiss on designing a flying-boat that would cross the Atlantic. The war killed the idea and brought Porte back to the Navy, but his association with Curtiss was kept up and encouraged. The Little America and Large America flying-boats were American in Design and conception and it was they that held back the Zeppelins and hit the U-boats. Before the war was over their *chef d'oeuvre,* the great triplane weighing 15 tons and called *Felixstowe Fury,* was in service with its five engines, four guns and great bomb-load. Nothing like it was seen again until the Flying Fortress took to the air twenty-odd years later.

The very success of the RNAS caused its rapid decline, for Mr. Churchill was beginning to find his own child an expensive luxury. For this he cannot be blamed. Russia was out, Italy and France were on the ropes, America was still largely in training and it was on the battered British Army that the outcome of the war depended. With men over middle age, men of low medical category and men already twice or thrice wounded being passed over to France with the greatest possible speed he was putting searching questions. How did the RNAS justify its size and costly gear? How many Zeppelins and submarines had it destroyed? In such accounts negatives, such as an unravaged countryside and a reasonably well fed people, cannot be figured. Had the war gone on into 1919 the RNAS would have been greatly trimmed down. Even as things stood, strength in pilots was only kept up by the attachment of a number of young Ensigns from the US Navy. They fitted into the squadrons and messes so happily that it was hard to believe that there had ever been a Revolutionary War. Potter, Keys, Eaton, Roe and Teulon were by common consent amongst the best of the Yarmouth flying sailors.

When Samson re-joined the days of the individual gladiator were over. This he well understood, feeling possibly much as Drake had done when reporting for duty under Lord Howard of Effingham. The command to which he succeeded at Yarmouth was running like a clock; the North Sea was cobwebbed into sectors and every interstice was marked in some fashion. Only one thing remained. All this was defensive warfare, waiting for the enemy to stick out his head and then hitting it. In spite of several false starts there was still no aircraft carrier fit to be so called, though Dunning and Rutland had demonstrated the possibility of using such a ship in conjunction with the Sopwith Pup. Once more Samson set himself the task of devising some workable expedient. It was not until May 1918, the awful period between the March Retreat and the advance to victory, when it seemed as if the war might after all be lost, that he was given his head. By then the RNAS had, on paper, become lost in the much greater RAF and Samson, after twenty years in the Navy, had to learn to call himself Colonel and salute with palm outwards. At òne thing he jibbed; his beard was an old friend, a trade-mark of long standing and without it he would be unrecognizable. Correspondence passed; the Air Ministry, possibly wishing to avoid offending the Royal Navy more than it had done by taking away its air arm, gave way gracefully. Colonel Samson might keep his beard, even though it would be the only one in the Force.

He confabulated with Admiral Sir Reginald Tyrwhitt, as much a thruster as himself, about the production of some ersatz carrier that would ferry fighters to within range of the German bases. The Zeebrugge raid on 23 April had not achieved what was hoped from it and Tyrwhitt was well disposed. There seemed one possibility, the big steel lighters that were used as rafts for flying-boats. On 30 May Samson set out to experiment. The lighter was coupled to a destroyer by a long tow-rope with a Sopwith Camel being held up in flying position with its undercarriage attached to skids. Off went the destroyer, working up to 30 knots as Samson sat in the cockpit warming up his engine. From there he could not see that the speed of the tug had pulled down the stern of the tow and his machine was pointing upwards at an angle of about 45 degrees. At a given signal it roared forward, one skid over-ran the trough and the Camel took off in a cart-wheel, falling into the sea a little ahead of the lighter. Down went the aircraft carrying Samson with it and the great pontoon, moving at unaccustomed speed on its own bow wave, passed overhead. Yet once more Samson's small frame proved no disadvantage. The cockpit of a Camel left a big man with hardly the room to scratch himself and in waterlogged flying kit no fourteen-stoner would have come up alive. An eye-witness, himself engaged in hanging on to the tail of the aircraft, expressed his feelings plainly. "I gasped and could not believe it possible that he would not be battered to atoms. It was all over in a second and before I had regained my legs the wreckage of the machine was 300 or 400 yards astern and no sign of Samson. Suddenly up bobbed a little white flying-cap and all heaved a sigh of relief . . . He was unhurt but had had a nasty time under the water disentangling himself from the wires of the wreck. The first thing he said as he ran nimbly up the side of the destroyers was: 'Well, Robertson, I think it well worth trying again.' " The skids, Samson's own idea, were taken away, the wheels put back and a young pilot named Culley repeated the performance. This time the launch was a complete success. Culley persevered and in August 1918 was towed on his lighter to a point some ten miles from the island of Borkum. His Camel took off and soon gained sufficient height to dive on and destroy a Zeppelin, something that no seaplane could do. When L53 hove in sight, comfortably secure in the knowledge that nothing would be able to touch her, Culley's guns opened up with long bursts of Pomeroy incendiary bullets and L53 went into the sea in flames. The Camel had to be ditched but it was a modest price to pay. Samson was well satisfied.

It was his last wartime exploit. With the Armistice the North Sea air stations were closed down; the men for the most part went home, the Americans officers returned to the US Navy and the aircraft were sold off. The Fleet Air Arm, when it came into being some years later, was always at the end of the queue for everything. Invention languished, every shilling was doled out as if it were the last one in the Treasury and the next war found the service with a collection of obsolete machines, most of which were already worn out. It was left to the navies of the United States and Japan to continue the business of making the air master of the sea.

Samson was made up to Group Captain RAF in October 1918; in 1920 he took over the Mediterranean Command and two years later was given his last promotion to Air Commodore.

The rest of Samson's story can be told shortly. In 1923 his marriage ended in divorce and, although he married again in the following year he seems never quite to have recovered from the blow. One last job, however, remained for the old buccaneer. In 1925 Captain Alan Cobham made his flight to the Cape, providing convincingly what the modern aeroplane could do. In the following year a complete bomber squadron took the same course across Africa, from Cairo to Capetown and back. Its leader was conspicuous for a small, neat beard, something rarely seen amongst the clean-shaven race of airmen. Two years later he retired and in 1931, at the early age of 48, Charles Rumney Samson died in his bed.

Jacky Fisher's New Navy, with its squadrons of great ships moving at speed and controlled by the orders of one man coming through the ether left no room for romance. One member, however, had had better luck. Coral islands and the singeing of the Kaiser's moustache came nearer in spirit to the age of the first Elizabeth than to the fifth George, but by happy coincidence here was a man who, navigating tiny under-powered craft through gales and darkness, was able to make the past live again.

CHAPTER EIGHT

"Lafayette, Me Voici!"

Raoul Lufbery

The Americans in Paris in August 1914 were as game as they were romantic. Alice Delysia's legs were amongst the glories of France; when she swung them on to a grand piano and burst into "La Marseillaise" there was only one thing a brave man could do. Since there was only one Corps that would accept aliens the younger men formed up to join it and as soon as the doors of the Foreign Legion recruiting office in the Rue des Enfants Abandonnes opened in the morning they crowded through it, to emerge as Soldats 2ième Classes.

None of the new Legionnaires had the slightest intention of wearing kepi, capote and pantalons rouges in desert stations far from the battlefields. Every one of them knew exactly what he wanted to do, and what he wanted to do was fly. Only Norman Prince knew anything about the subject, but they were popular young men with the right friends and by means into which it is profitless to enquire they were accepted for training. By the spring of 1915 the seven who survived the course found themselves sergeant-pilots in the French service, part of the Escadrille de Chasse Spad 124. With an eye to the strong German element in the States that objected to American citizens bearing arms against the Fatherland they adopted the name of Lafayette, as a reminder of the country that had helped in achieving their own independence. Their sign, painted on every machine, was an Indian's head. The French, hard pressed, were glad to indulge them and more and more young men, mostly fresh from the universities, crossed the Atlantic to join their friends. The idea caught on at home, was taken up by newspapers, and a Lafayette Flying Corps Committee, including men of the stature of ex-President Theodore Roosevelt, was formed to back them up. One American, however, already had his wandering days behind him and was on the spot.

Raoul Gervais Victor Lufbery had been born at Clermont in the Department of the Oise on 21 March 1885, the son of Edward Lufbery, late of New York, and Antoinette Vessières, his wife. Soon after the birth of Raoul his mother died, his father wasted no time over finding a new wife and, accompanied by her, returned to the United States where he went into business as a dealer in rare postage stamps. Raoul, with his two brothers, was left behind in the care of Antoinette's mother. The details of his next few years are scanty but some things are certain. His education was that of an ordinary French boy, but he had the advantage of being equally at home in French and English. The household of Mme. Vessières was miserably poor and at an early age Raoul was set to work in the Menier chocolate factory on the outskirts of the town of Blois, dominated by the great castle in which Catherine de Medici had died. After a spell there he moved on to a job with one of the factories in the industrial centre of Clermont-Ferrand which was to France what Essen was to Germany. At 19 Raoul had had enough of factory hooters and boring, repetitive work and decided to seek his fortune abroad. First he went to Algiers; finding nothing there to grip him, he moved on to Tunis and thence to Cairo. Exactly how he supported himself is not clear but as some of his future occupations included bar-tending and waiting it seems probable that he was known in the kitchens and dining-rooms of the better hotels. From Cairo he travelled to Turkey where, as he later said, he found a job as a waiter in Constantinople which he held down long enough to pick up a working knowledge of Turkish. Then, bored again, he travelled through the Balkans to Germany, where the Woermann Line was glad to find a place for an American citizen with a good command of languages. The job opened up opportunities of further travel and Raoul decided that he might turn it to advantage by seeking out his missing father. In 1906 he turned up at the scene of Edward Lufbery's last known place of abode, Wallingford, Connecticut, only to find that the second Mrs. Lufbery was dead in her turn and that Edward, with yet another wife, had returned to France. It does not seem that Raoul ever came across his father again; no doubt he was able to bear this with his accustomed fortitude.

Having come so far, he felt no inclination to return to Europe, though he was entirely without means. Unperturbed, he buckled down and took a job in a silversmith's shop at Wallingford where he remained for the next two years. Then, once more, his feet began to itch. He tried Cuba, for all practical purposes an American colony, but he did not linger there; in a short time he was back in New Orleans acquiring a new skill by working in a bakery. This, too, failed to enchant him; he removed to San Francisco and resumed his old trade as a waiter. Being the cheerful, pleasant young man he was, he probably made an excellent one.

It was in San Francisco that he seems to have decided that it was time for him to settle down, at any rate for a little while. There he enlisted in the US Army and was at once posted to the Philippines. It was a rough time, for the Mohammedan part of the population was still in revolt and murders of unwary American soldiers were commonplace. Doubtless Raoul did his bit towards "civilizing them with a Krag". His three-year engagement, however, seems to have been uneventful, even if it was not particularly enjoyable. When it expired he did not re-enlist but took his discharge and went to see more of the world. He spent some time in Japan, travelled in China, and eventually turned up as a ticket-collector at Bombay's Victoria Station. In later years he claimed that he had never been without work of some kind for more than a week. When the delights of Bombay, such as they are, began to pall he took the train to Calcutta and there his purpose in life was revealed to him.

A number of early French aviators took their machines into places far from Europe in the hope, usually vain, of finding markets for them. M. Ollivier went to Egypt, where he gave Lord Kitchener his first and only flight, over the Pyramids. Marc Pourpre decided to try India. At the moment that Raoul Lufbery left the train at Howrah Station he was giving exhibition flights in a Bleriot from the Maidan and was suddenly grounded by the defection of his mechanic. Lufbery volunteered to fill the vacancy and Pourpre, enchanted at finding a half-Frenchman with some mechanical knowledge, took him on. Together they toured the sub-continent, the pilot steadily teaching his new friend more and more about the workings of the early aeroplane engine. From India they travelled to Saigon and thence to Cairo, where Pourpre flew up the Nile to Khartoum and back.

By the merest chance the two of them were in Paris in August 1914, waiting to take delivery of a new machine. On the declaration of war Pourpre instantly formed up to the War Office and was given a commission in the flying service. Raoul, still an American citizen – he must have renounced his dual nationality on joining the US Army – did what other Americans did and joined the Legion, though wires were at once pulled and he found himself transferred to the air corps, still grinding valves and cleaning the plugs on Pourpre's machine. Before 1914 was out Lufbery's friend was dead, shot down in battle, and his mechanic decided to avenge him. Still Soldat 2ième classe, he volunteered for training as a pilot and was accepted, going to the Aviation School at Chartres and from there being passed on to Voisin Bombardment Squadron No. 106. Throughout 1915 and early 1916 he flew his bomber without anything spectacular happening. Then, in February 1916, came Verdun.

This, after the Marne, was the decisive battle of the war and, notwithstanding the dismal events of 1940, it is the abiding glory of the French Army. Everything that Germany could amass was brought to the valley of the Woevre with the object of bleeding the French Army white. Russia was reeling, the British Army had not yet appeared in full strength and the prospect of America ceasing to be too proud to fight seemed non-existent. France, feeling very much alone, took the full weight of the German blows. Only the occasional sight of an Indian head on the fuselage of a Spad, usually being flown with a splendid recklessness, gave the poilu cause to remember that his country still had friends. The first casualty of the Lafayette came in May, when the battle was at its height; in the last week of that terrible month his replacement arrived, Serjeant Raoul Lufbery, late of the Legion.

An official photograph taken at about this time shows Lufbery as all Auvergnat in appearance, short, thick-set, heavily-moustached and with crisp black hair cut *en brosse*. Behind the official scowl, obligatory at such moments, there appears a strong square face that might break into a broad grin at any moment. The names of Nordhoff and Hall suggest their admirable book *Mutiny on the Bounty* but long before that appeared in print the two men had collaborated in bringing out a history of the Lafayette Flying Corps, of which Hall was a distinguished member. They make it plain that "Luf" was the best-loved of them all, loved for his cheerful engaging personality, his complete lack of swank and utter fearlessness in the air. Two lion cubs named Whiskey and Soda were the Squadron's mascots; they roamed where they pleased and, while both were Lufbery's cronies. Soda became particularly attached to him, knew the sound of his engine and always waited impatiently for his *aterrissage*. The other characteristic noted by Hall was a passion for mushrooms, the search for which seems to have taken up most of his leisure time.

Lufbery's fame spread beyond the American squadron to the best of the Frenchmen, for the Lafayette shared Bar-le-Duc aerodrome with the Escadrille de Chasse No. 3, led by Georges Guynemer and including amongst its pilots Rene Fonck, Père Dorme, and Navarre. Their stork badge, the Cigogne (you

can still see it on Hispano-Suiza cars), was the most famous
sign throughout the French service and rivalry between stork
and Indian head was intense. It was the French who introduced the word "ace", signifying a pilot with five confirmed
victories, to the language. In the German service ten victories
made a pilot a "kanone"; the British discouraged the whole
business as unseemly, but an ace in France was a popular
hero.

Lufbery qualified very quickly. The French history tells of it,
though without much detail. "Fearless and handling his plane
with superb mastery and ease, he was soon acknowledged best
of them all (in the Lafayette). There was no love of the spectacular or the heroic in him, only keen zest for flying and simple
devotion to his work." Captain Georges Therault, his Commanding Officer, wrote that: "Above all the pilots who found
themselves at Verdun, Lufbery was 'sans peur et sans
reproche'. His Spad was always the highest and every day he
won new victories. He seemed hardly to care about having
them confirmed. Calmly he reigned as sovereign lord in his
chosen element and beat down his foes to accomplish his duty
and not for the sake of glory." Officially he was credited with
seventeen victories, "though he undoubtedly brought down
twice that number". Nor were these the kind of scores notched
up by pouncing from a great height upon unsuspecting two-
seaters. The French Army, fighting as never before or since,
depended largely upon its guns and everything had to be
sacrificed in order to keep them trained on their targets. French
reconnaissance aircraft, knowing themselves to be sitting
ducks, never failed their artillery, flying out again and again to
find the co-ordinates the gunlayers needed. German pilots
strained every nerve to knock them down and, though they had
many successes, they paid a heavy price for them as
Guynemer, Lufbery, Fonck, Prince and the rest threw their
little chasers about the sky like wheeling kites. Spad and Fokker were pretty evenly matched and neither was an easy
machine to fly. Many French pilots, transferred from the
cavalry, insisted on retaining their spurs. When asked why, the

invariable answer was: "Fly a Spad and you will see for yourself".

As all the world knows, the French Army held fast and the war was not lost. The cost was appalling, and France has never quite recovered from it. To this day there are swathes of earth where nothing will grow and once thriving villages are lost for ever in a jungle. The Lafayette Flying Corps was hit as hard as any. By the end of 1916, when it moved from Verdun to Cachy, only one of the seven remained. At the Armistice forty Americans had died fighting under the sign of the Indian's head. Lufbery's prowess was recognized with the Legion of Honour and Medaille Militaire, the Croix de Guerre with ten palms and the British Military Medal. In addition he was, whatever his citizenship might have been, commissioned sous-lieutenant in August 1917. Throughout America his was the biggest name in flying and the newspapers took him up joyfully.

When the United States entered the war their Army had no air branch worth mentioning and efforts were made to get Raoul back under his own colours. The decision was a hard one for him but on 10 January 1918 he became Major Lufbery of the US Signal Corps in command of a Squadron. The outlook was bleak, for America was surprisingly unready. In 1865 the United States had possessed the most powerful army in the world, stronger by far than that of Bismarck's Prussia. Soon, as Mr. Longfellow had said, "the warrior's name would be a name abhorred" and in a few years it all fell away. The rough levies raised for Mr. Hearst's "splendid little war" of 1898 did nothing to raise the warrior's status and in 1916 the US Army could hardly have taken on a large banana republic with certainty of success. Its industry, led by Mr. Schwab of Bethlehem Steel, had long been at work for the Allies but when the AEF reached France it had hardly a weapon of its own beyond an insufficient number of '03-pattern rifles. The legacy of the Wrights had vanished, for, apart from some Curtiss naval machines, no American fighting aeroplane existed. For artillery, tanks and aircraft the US had to depend upon what Britain and France could spare. As the RFC was, by 1918, twice the size of the French service many American pilots and mechanics moved in bodily with it. Others, who had long regarded the Lafayette as the vanguard of an American Flying Corps, made up new squadrons, lacking everything but biding their time.

"Luf" was first assigned to Squadron 95, where his battle kit consisted of a roll-top desk and a pencil. Soon he was passed on to 94, a little more promising as it had a few Nieuports and pilots who included Edward Rickenbacker and Quentin Roosevelt, but not a single machine-gun. Throughout that terrible March when German armies drove towards Paris in the hope of winning the war before America could make her presence felt, he was of little use to either of his countries and could only fret. This time it was the turn of the British Army to "cramponner partout" and, as France had held at Verdun, so did Britain and the old Empire hold now. By April Lufbery was in the air again, still gunless but training his young lions to fight as the Lafayette had fought. Rickenbacker has testified that they almost worshipped this squat little man and tried to imitate him in everything. In the States he had been a national hero since before April 1917 and the newspapers were awaiting his further feats.

The US service followed the practice of the RFC by not using parachutes. Sholto Douglas, writing in 1963, said that "to put it mildly, it would have been a great comfort to us to have had such a means of escape to rely on in emergencies, and it would certainly have saved many men from horrible deaths. It was not until a few months ago that I learnt to my disgust that the reason why we did not have them was an astonishing policy during the First World War that deliberately denied us the use of parachutes." The reason, "that pilots would have been encouraged to leave their machines", was insulting and its source has never been traced. Douglas, than whom nobody had a better right to speak, called it "a contemptible decision". Talk in 94's Mess often turned upon what a man should do if his machine caught fire. Lufbery's advice was firm. Never jump, for that way you have no chance at all. Stay in the machine and try to steer a course that will stream the flames away from you until you get down somehow. Also pray.

By May, Squadron 95 had received its guns and was operational, flying over the old 1870 battlefields around Metz. Lufbery was happy again, and devoted all his attention to teaching eager young men their trade. Once more he shot down a German two-seater and all looked set for further victories. On 19 May 1918 a single German aeroplane came unscathed through the French anti-aircraft fire and prowled overhead. Lufbery, vexed at such insolence, dashed up on a motor-cycle and demanded his Nieuport to be rolled out. The mechanic told him that it was under repair; as another was standing by Lufbery scrambled into it and was off. At 2,000 feet, as the Squadron watched in hope of seeing another quick kill, the two machines closed and short bursts of machine-gun fire could be plainly heard. Then, very suddenly, came gasps of horror as flames leapt from the Nieuport's engine and swept down on to the pilot. No spin, side-slip, loop or any of the manoeuvres in which Lufbery was so skilled could turn the fire away from him and in an instant the watchers saw a figure emerge from the cockpit and jump; it twisted in the air and then fell like a dead thing to the earth below.

Rickenbacker was the first to arrive in the cottage garden where peasants were reverently laying out the charred and twisted body, one hand bleeding from a bullet that had carried away the thumb. It seemed beyond belief that "Luf" was dead. "He was America's Ace of Aces," wrote Rickenbacker, and it was true. Had there been time for an American Air Force to grow in a size comparable with the others Raoul Lufbery would have been its fighting commander. As things were the torch passed to Rickenbacker, who carried it high.

They gave Raoul a great military funeral, Generals Gèrard and Hunter Liggett attending along with Colonel Billy Mitchell. In the States he was mourned as if a battle had been lost. On 14 July, of all days, Theodore Roosevelt's son Quentin joined him.

All good Americans when they die are said to go to Paris. One good American will never leave the city. On 14 July 1928 all that was mortal of Raoul Lufbery was taken from the American Cemetery and re-interred with his comrades in the Lafayette Squadron Memorial at Villeneuve. Lafayette would have acknowledged the debt paid.

CHAPTER NINE

The Gasman Cometh

Frank Luke

By the summer of 1918 the balloon was a little out of date as a weapon of war. Napoleon and Ulysses Grant had found it useful, Lord Roberts had employed it once in South Africa and when the rival armies sank into the ground towards the end of 1914 it seemed entirely natural that it should come into service again. Thought had been given to means of blinding it, for long before the war the firm of Krupp had been advertising a "balloon-gun"; it does not seem to have attracted many purchasers. Certainly, in a quieter age, the balloon had had advantages over other forms of horizon-widening. Lord Kitchener himself had made an ascent in one during his brief service with the French Army in 1870 and the cold had nearly killed him. When the first armed aeroplane arrived the days of the balloon seemed numbered but until an acceptable substitute could be found it was worth persevering with the thing.

As a bag full of highly inflammable gas anchored to the ground at the end of a wire cable seemed an unmissable target, much ingenuity was exercised in protecting them. At this the Germans excelled, with batteries of the rockets known as "flaming onions", groups of anti-aircraft guns cunningly sited and little traps made up of baskets of explosives electrically detonated as soon as the unsuspecting aircraft was lured near enough. On the other side men tried the Hales grenade – useless, because it slid off – and various forms of incendiary bullet known as Buckingham and Pomeroy. There were Le Prieur rockets fired from wing-tips, large fish-hooks to be trailed over the fabric and rip it to pieces and many crafty devices of private manufacture. One thing became clear early on. Destroying balloons looks as if it must be safe and easy; experience showed it to be difficult, dangerous and a job to be avoided if at all possible. Then there was the question of public attitudes; if a man shot down another aeroplane he was a hero, but to shoot down a balloon sounded, except to the cognoscenti, almost like a joke.

A few eccentrics, however, decided that the igniting of such things was their purpose in life. Willy Coppens, the renowned Belgian pilot, touched off twenty-six of them; Roth, the German, announced that he was so bad a shot that he would have to concentrate on balloons and accounted for seventeen. Beauchamp-Proctor, possibly the best of the many South Africans in the RFC, scored one less. Frank Luke, of the United States Army, tied with Coppens but as he also had an impressive score amongst the German aeroplanes he should be given the lead on points.

Luke was born in Phoenix, Arizona in 1897; his ancestry was pure German, for his father had come from Prussia and his mother's family were descended from the first German settlers on Long Island. His own general appearance proclaimed Nordic ancestry, but there all connection ended and the Lukes had become patriotic Americans. His education was scanty but he was put to work earlier than most boys and grew up a rugged young man. How Luke came to be interested in flying is unclear but it was to the Signal Corps that he reported soon after his enlistment in June 1917. It is reasonable to suppose that tales of Prince, Lufbery and the other grandees of the Lafayette had caught his imagination as they caught those of most American boys of his time, but this can only be guesswork. Be that as it may, he certainly went early to the flying school at Rockwell Field, San Diego, where he gained his wings and a commission. At this time he must have been tractable enough, for he passed through his course without much difficulty, but it soon became plain that the eighteen-year-old had not inherited the best-known German quality. Frank Luke hated discipline; it was fashionable amongst young men, and not only amongst American young men, to assert their independence by proclaiming loudly that such a slavery was not for them, but most soon grew out of it. Luke never did. Perhaps matters would have fallen out differently had his flying career begun at another time but it was July 1918 when he disembarked in France and by then the Allied air forces undoubtedly held the upper hand. Risks that would have been considered criminal a year earlier could now be taken with impunity.

Perhaps also he was unlucky in his beginnings. His first commanding officer was a Canadian, Major Hartney, who had flown with No. 20 Squadron RFC and was held in great respect; he was beginning to get it into Luke's head that the days of Albert Ball and Raoul Lufbery had become history and that flying now was team-work, to be carried out in well-trained formations. Luke was grudgingly coming round to believing this when Hartney was moved away and a new commander arrived whose only merit was that he was American. Luke seems to have taken a dislike to him and set himself out to display his contempt for the system. Formation flying bored him, the Spad with its 220 hp engine was irresistible and Luke, whenever he felt like it, broke away and looked for trouble. Very soon he found it; he came home with his Spad riddled almost to pieces and a story, quickly confirmed, of a shot-down German. When the Squadron, the 27th, moved to a field near Verdun his Flight Commander, who had had enough of Luke's little ways, grounded him. Shooting down an enemy aircraft was too commonplace an achievement now for it to outweigh deliberate defiance of orders. Luke sulked, grumbled and meditated spectacular revenge.

On 21 September the American offensive in the Argonne opened; when nobody was looking, Luke climbed into an unattended Spad and set off. A balloon seemed a promising target and he went for it; the balloon-men were old hands at the game and promptly hauled it down. Luke dived after it and pressed the trigger of his machine-gun; nothing happened. In a flurry of bad words he pulled the Spad up and tried again; by the time he was back the balloon was nearly on the ground but Luke was not letting it go. This time the gun fired, the balloon caught flame (surprisingly, as he was using ordinary ammunition) and dropped neatly on top of its winch. Luke narrowly missed hitting the ground but managed to get away well peppered by fire from all round him. What passed between him and Captain Grant is not recorded, but two days later he was sent off with orders to destroy another one, over Buzy.

Luke does not seem to have been over-popular – he was a roughish diamond compared to most of the American pilots – but in Joseph Wehner he had one close friend. Wehner was also of German stock and the two men had met during training; when Grant asked Luke who he would like to cover him for this task there was only one possible choice. Wehner's Spad kept an entire flight of Fokkers in play while Luke attended to the business. He shot down his balloon and, finding this too tame for an afternoon's work set off to find another and destroyed that also. The sight of so much burning gas – enough to cook the dinners of a good-sized town – must have been satisfying and both Luke and Wehner decided that they must have more of it. Next day they roamed around Verdun and picked off three. This time they were expected and seven Fokkers set about them. While they were attending to Luke, Wehner got himself into a good firing position and shot down two. As the others made off Luke decided that he could employ the rest of the afternoon profitably and sped off to shoot down another balloon, somewhere to the north of Verdun. While he was so engaged Wehner got into a fight with another eight Fokkers who were pestering an American observation machine. Once again he chose his position nicely, shot down one, drove down another and shepherded the two-seater home. Luke joined him on the ground but soon they became bored again. Wehner took his bet, that he could knock down three more balloons before sunset, and off they went again. Luke won his wager.

They had a few days' rest after this but on 20 September were at it again. Two balloons at Labeuville invited attention and as Luke was burning them up Wehner occupied the attention of the fighters. Luke, glancing up, saw six of them buzzing round his friend and rushed up to join in. He shot down two in rapid succession but as soon as he was free to look round he found the sky empty. That the Fokkers had made off was not surprising, but of Wehner also there was no trace. Luke turned for home, absent-mindedly wiping the eyes of a flight of French Spads hunting a two-seater by shooting it down as he passed.

Wehner was dead, brought down in his last unequal fight by the guns of the Fokkers. His career had been brief, but he had taken eight of the enemy with him. Luke, bereft of his only friend, was inconsolable; he had always been a prickly young man but now he became a savage. A hatred for the Germans who had killed Wehner filled his mind to the exclusion of all else and it is not a healthy state for a professional fighting man. He began to cut his routine duties and Captain Grant weakly let him get away with it. He got into the habit of taking his Spad off on private adventures, apparently caring little whether he killed or was killed. The balloons seemed to be the concentrated object of his hate and he hunted them relentlessly. Whilst under arrest, for the crime of leaving the aerodome without orders, landing at a French field and staying there without bothering to tell anybody, he walked to his Spad and took off without a word in search of some more.

Luke's last flight was a piece of pure bravado. As the sun was setting he dropped a message over the American headquarters at Souilly, saying succinctly, "Watch three Hun balloons along the Meuse. Luke." This produced a substantial audience for the Wagnerian end. First, the balloon over Dun-sur-Meuse broke into the usual pillar of flames, moments later the one over Briere Farm went the same way. Then came a pause, the typewriter-noise of machine-guns plainly heard through the

summer night; then came the third flash and roar. Only afterwards did the watchers understand what they had seen. Between the first and the second balloons the Fokkers had caught
up with Luke; by the time he wrecked the second he had taken
a bullet in the body, before reaching the third he was badly
wounded but still capable of flying his damaged plane and
firing his gun. The last balloon, over Milly, he had nearly
rammed before dodging past it as it burned. Then he flew on,
faintly and with his sight failing, until he was over the German
position in the village of Murvaux. With his last strength he
raked the street with his machine-gun; then he crash-landed by
the church. The German infantry closed in but Luke had not
yet done with them. With praeternatural fortitude he dragged
his broken body into the churchyard, found cover behind a
tomb and fished out his Colt ·45 pistol. The Germans, decent
men, invited him to surrender. Luke's reply was to open up
with his pistol; being left with no choice, a German soldier shot
him dead. Frank Luke may not have been a particularly nice
man, but what a way to go out!

Amongst the old Germanic tribes there was a tradition of
blood-brotherhood, each under oath not to return alone.
Perhaps this had something to do with what was surely a
spectacular suicide. Perhaps it was sheer bad temper. Whatever the reason, Frank Luke remains the first airman to whom
the Congressional Medal of Honor has been awarded post-
humously. With eighteen victories, additional to his balloons,
he ranks second to Rickenbacker with twenty six at the top of
the US averages. And all of it was done in a matter of a few
weeks.

CHAPTER TEN

The Fist of Uncle Sam

James H. Doolittle

In that fine novel *Mr. Standfast*, the last of the trilogy begun with the *Thirty Nine Steps*, John Buchan describes a conversation between his hero Richard Hannay, now a General, and his American co-adjutor John S. Blenkiron. The date is late March 1918 and the place near Amiens. "We passed a company of American soldiers, and Blenkiron had to stop and stare. I could see that he was stiff with pride, though he wouldn't show it. 'What d'you think of that bunch?' he asked. 'First-rate stuff,' I said. 'The men are all right,' he drawled critically, 'but some of the officer-boys are a bit puffy. They want fining down.' 'They'll get it soon enough, honest fellows. You don't keep your weight long in this war.' 'Say, Dick,' he said shyly, 'what do you think of our Americans? You've seen a lot of them and I'd value your views.' 'I'll tell you what I think. You're constructing a great middle-class army, and that's the most formidable fighting-machine on earth. This kind of war doesn't want the Berserker so much as the quiet fellow with a trained mind and a lot to fight for. The American ranks are filled with all sorts, from cow-punchers to college boys, but mostly with decent lads that have good prospects in life before them and are fighting because they feel bound to, not because they like it. It was the same stock that pulled through in your Civil War.' " Buchan wrote of what he had seen, and he seen much of armies.

Such a one was James H. Doolittle. In his small form – at five feet three inches he was about the same size as Samson – were concentrated the qualities of both cow-puncher and college boy, for he gained experience young. When he was born in 1896 his father was engaged in business activities that took him on travels between his home in California and the Yukon goldfields. Jimmy, though born too late to have been a genuine sourdough or to have witnessed the shooting of Dan McGrew, grew up in Nome, a place of little refinement, and there he learnt early how to fight. He became a boxer of repute and had he had been a head taller he might easily have turned professional. The first money he made was certainly earned with his fists.

He returned to Los Angeles and a more sheltered life in the years soon after the Wright brothers had made every adventurous young man to lift up his eyes far above the hills, and the infection never left him. Even as he was working his way through high school and the University of California he experimented, inside the limits of his narrow means, with the building of aeroplanes that never flew, although his formal education was directed to becoming a mining engineer. In 1917 he naturally got himself into the Signal Corps, the parent body of the US Army Air Corps, and became a pilot. In a way his fitness for the job was his undoing for he soon became a flier of rare quality and the authorities reckoned that he would be more usefully employed in training others than in taking his place in a squadron in France. He is said to have had a strong sense of fun which got him into trouble from time to time, a circumstance easy to believe, but his flying skill was such that he always escaped serious trouble.

When the war ended, Doolittle remained in the Army, but not to moulder in garrison towns waiting for the slow process of promotion. America was ripe for the opening up of air routes, but it was an expensive business and the Army, now underemployed, was put to use in developing the new form of communication. Lieutenant Doolittle was chosen in 1922 to make the first coast-to-coast flight across the continent and accomplished it with his usual efficiency. His reward was to be given every opportunity to perfect himself in aerobatics and to teach the new pilots to carry out the most complicated loops, rolls and turns in formation. He became well-known as a result of the subsequent newspaper publicity but it was not until 1925 that his name became famous outside North America.

M. Schneider had presented his Trophy in 1913 for a speed competition between seaplanes of any nationality, and since Prevost had won the first race at an average speed of a little over 45 mph it had become much more than a mere sporting event. Mussolini's Italy set great store by the prestige that would come to any really spectacular performance and Italian aircraft were very good indeed. What had once been a private amusement became an affair of governments. For comparatively small outlay they could run a kind of friendly war while improving the breed of fast aircraft in the process. France, Italy and Britain had all won the Trophy at various times, but never the country that had produced the first flying-machine. This was not to be endured, especially as the 1925 event was to be held in Chesapeake Bay. The Curtiss Company entered a machine under US colours, and as Doolittle happened to be away from the Army, doing a three year course at the Massachusetts Institute of Technology on aeronautical engineering, he was readily available to fly it.

The Navy was not over-pleased at an Army pilot flying a seaplane but Doolittle was forgiven his presumption when he won, at a speed of over 200 mph. The Schneider Trophy results were eagerly followed all over the world, every wireless station keeping up a regular flow of bulletins, and the unusual name was heard coming over the ether from every point on the dial. When it became famous for another reason it was not the name of a stranger.

Mr. Keyes, chairman of the Curtiss-Wright Company, took all this in and sensibly made the best use he could of it. With the Army's blessing Jimmy turned salesman, demonstrating the virtues of the Curtiss range of aircraft throughout South America; his low-level aerobatics were enjoyed in many countries south of the Rio Grande and his friends now numbered rich men with no service connections. It is fair to suppose that his income was no longer limited to a Lieutenant's miserable pay. On 24 September 1929, on loan to the Sperry Gyroscope Company, Doolittle made the first test of instrument flying, using a gyro horizon, directional gyro and the Kollsman altimeter but denied vision by the black hood clamped firmly over his cockpit. The take-off, flight and landing were all carried out faultlessly and no longer did a pilot need to rely on his eyes alone. Only a man of the highest quality and much self-confidence would have dared make the attempt; only a pilot of quintessential skill could have carried it out successfully.

His future, at 34, now plainly lay outside the Army and in 1930 Doolittle resigned his commission in order to join the Shell Company. Under this sponsorship he made a record-breaking flight across America in 1931 – the year in which the RAF won the Schneider Trophy outright (the film *Hell's Angel* revived for many memories of war-time flying) and followed it up with the world's speed record for land-planes in 1932. In 1935 he set up another, this time for the longest non-stop flight by a commercial plane across the USA. Shell lent him back to Curtiss and he became their chief demonstrator of military aircraft in Europe. Probably his most important work at this time was in the matter of aviation fuel, little changed since 1918. It had become clear that the piston-engine was by then as near perfection as it would ever be and only by better spirit could its performance be improved. The higher-compression engines were not yet in wide use and the cost of turning out the 100-octane petrol which they needed would be enormous. It was Doolittle, with unequalled prestige behind him, who persuaded the great Shell company to sink about two million dollars into this unpromising commercial venture; without it the aircraft of the Allies would, in a few years' time, have been at a serious disadvantage as against the Luftwaffe.

In 1940, scenting war in the offing, Doolittle rejoined the

Army and was promoted to Lieutenant-Colonel at a bound. Then came Pearl Harbor. It was the humiliation, possibly more even than the loss, that set America by the ears. Nobody seriously contemplated defeat but such an affront could not await vengeance during the long time that would be needed in organizing America for full-scale war. President Roosevelt took counsel as to what could be done at once to hit back and his Air Force chief, General Arnold, recommended the pressing into service of James H. Doolittle. No man could have been better fitted for the task, even though the Navy could hide its enthusiasm at the job being given to a soldier.

First it was necessary to consider what weapons were at hand for the chastisement. The Navy still had two excellent carriers, *Hornet* and *Enterprise*; the Army had a number of good bombing aircraft, of which the B25, the Mitchell, was reckoned the best. The immediate need was to work out means by which the two could be combined, for carriers were not built to fly off lumbering great aircraft nor were bombers designed to carry fuel for a couple of thousand miles in addition to their ordinary loads. Chiang Kai Shek, while not taken entirely into the President's confidence, agreed to put airfields in China at America's disposal on the understanding that the machines would remain there for him to use after they had done their work.

Doolittle worked out the details; he would need twenty-four Mitchells, each modified to carry a total of 1,141 gallons of fuel and a bomb-load of 2,000 lb. It could be done, just, by turning each bomber into a flying tanker with rubber bags in the crawlways and drums wedged in wherever a crevice could be found. Thus loaded the machines could only operate at low level but that would be sufficient. In order to save weight the ·50-calibre machine-guns facing the rear must go, being replaced by light wooden mock-ups. Sperry bomb-sights were too important to be risked; out they went and in came a home-made affair called Mark Twain. Next he called for volunteers to make up his five man crews. It was impossible to tell them for what they were volunteering but they came just the same; there was no hand-picking; just ordinary, average crews. February of 1942 was spent at Eglin Field in Florida, practising day in and day out the art of getting a B25 weighing 31,000 lb. into the air without over-running the area marked out to the size and shape of a carrier's deck. After that they practised aiming and releasing bombs from 1,500 feet, followed by the quickest climb possible.

While his crews practised, Doolittle did sums. The ideal would be to steam within 450 miles of the Japanese coast without being spotted; 550 would serve, but 650 was the absolute limit.

By the end of March he was satisfied and twenty-two of the original twenty-four Mitchells flew from Florida to the Alameda Naval Air Station at San Francisco where USS *Hornet* awaited them. Chiang Kai Shek was now privy to the plan and had promised to have fuel and flares ready at Kweilin, Kian, Yushan, and Chuchow, on a roughly east-west line south of Shanghai. Once *Hornet* was at sea there could be no further communication with him, for absolute wireless silence was essential. On 1 April the Navy hoisted the Army bombers, now reduced to sixteen for reasons of space, on board *Hornet* and lashed them down on the flight deck. Next day she steamed through the Golden Gate to join Admiral Halsey in the carrier *Enterprise* off Midway.

It was a rough passage; the Mitchells were crammed together with the rearmost hanging over *Hornet*'s counter and the crews, now well aware of what they had volunteered to do, found little to enjoy. Task Force 16, as the whole was called, joined its two parts together without incident and set course for Japan. There are substantial differences between the official accounts by the two services of what happened next. The date was 18 April 1942 and it was certainly in the early hours of the morning that a Japanese patrol boat was picked up on *Hornet*'s radar. The Admiral, with America's only surviving carrier force under his hand, was not going to endanger it for a mere gesture of defiance. The Army account says that the order to fly off was given at 0800 hrs. with 800 miles of sea between the ships and the target. Admiral Morison, in the Navy's tale, says that take-off began at 0725 at a distance of 623 miles from the Japenese coast and 668 from Tokio. Whichever is right it was greatly in excess of the most pessimistic of Doolittle's calculations, and verging on the impossible. Nevertheless, he did not hesitate for a moment. It was not only a matter of national pride; for the Navy to return home and announce that the Army had been unwilling to play would have been beyond human endurance.

Doolittle's plane, the leader, had 467 feet of deck in which to get itself airborne. The weather was awesome, a 40-knot half-gale making *Hornet* pitch enough to ship green sea over the flight deck with frightening regularity. No twin-engined bomber had ever before taken off from a carrier even in ideal conditions; a single electrical spark in the wrong place would have sent everything and everybody skyward in a titanic funeral pyre. Admiral Halsey wrote his own account of the departure. "When Doolittle's plane buzzed down *Hornet*'s deck at 0725 there wasn't a man topside in Task Force 16 who didn't help him sweat into the air. One pilot hung on the brink of a stall until we nearly catalogued his effects, but the last of the 16 was airborne by 0824." The forced departure from the time table was serious. They would probably now arrive over the Chinese airfields, if they arrived at all, in the dark, and, loaded as they were, the Mitchells were in no shape to put up much of a fight if the Japanese Navy Zeros found them. The Army pilots shifted their gum and addressed themselves to navigation.

Doolittle crossed the coast at noon and a few minutes later the enemy's capital lay beneath him. By the merest fluke its inhabitants were engaged in a practice alert and they took no particular notice of the arrival of Nemesis. No fighter appeared, nor was there any immediate anti-aircraft fire. Doolittle released his cluster of incendiaries exactly where he had intended. Lieutenant Hoover, next astern, dropped to 900 feet and let go both incendiaries and three 500 lb demolition

target, the oil stores and factory areas. Three visited the real
enemy, the Imperial Navy yards at Yokohama, Kobe and
Yokosuka where Lieutenant McElroy scored a direct hit on the
carrier Ryuho. There was some anti-aircraft fire around these
places but only one bomber was hit and that not seriously. A
few fighters put in an appearance but they were no Kamikazes.
The sight of the wooden machine-guns seemed to discourage
them.

So far all had gone very satisfactorily, though it was undeni-
able that bombs had fallen on some residential areas, but the
worst of the voyage was to come. From Tokio to the nearest
Chinese airfield was about 1,100 miles and even with the
friendly tail wind it was doubtful whether any of them would
see home again. Thick dark clouds built up over the Yellow
Sea and some of the engines were showing that they had not
been improved by a long, wet sea passage, and the fuel-gauge
needles dropped at frightening speed. As night came down the
American crews battled on towards China, hoping for the best
but far from expecting it. The Chinese, unaware of what had
happened, extinguished their flares on hearing engines in the
belief that this was a raid, and there was little to be seen but
black, menacing cloud above and more blackness below. One
Mitchell, its engines at their last gasp, made for Vladivostok
and Russian hospitality. It landed safely but it was more than a
year before the crew turned up again in Persia with a story to
tell. Four of the pilots, including Doolittle, managed to crash-
land at Chuchow without injury, their last drop of fuel gone,
while the other eleven crashed in various places. Of fifty men
who parachuted down into China, forty-nine were led to safety
by peasants, the other being killed during the descent. Three
who survived a drop into Japanese-held territory were tried
and shot, one died in prison and four were released after the
war. Of the eighty who set out from *Hornet*, seventy-one survived. Not a single Mitchell remained to take service under the
Chinese. The losses seemed heavy, for America was not yet
blooded; by European standards they were trivial. The result
was well worth while, not only because it compelled Japan to

keep at home fighter squadrons soon to be badly needed in the Solomons, but because it had been a gesture of rare spirit mingled with a strong element of mystery. Uncle Sam spat on his hands and looked the world in the eye again. The old recruiting poster proclaiming: "Cheer up. Nobody's ever licked HIM" was no longer a mockery.

It is commonly believed that the Army and the Navy of the United States economize on mutual admiration. When Admiral Halsey wrote that "in my opinion their flight was one of the most courageous deeds in all military history", it was a compliment worth having. Nor would many disagree with it.

The Tokio raid sent Lieutenant-Colonel Doolittle rocketing to the top of the Air Corps, and when Torch, the North African landing, was in the planning stage he seemed far and away the best qualified man to run the air side of it. His appointment was not unopposed, for no army enthuses about a man who has left its ranks in order to become a rich civilian. Eisenhower, himself about to see his first battle, did not want him and said so; in the end he yielded to the persuasion of General Arnold and took Brigadier-General Doolittle as head of the American air forces in the field. He never regretted the decision and, with characteristic generosity, was not slow to admit that he had under-rated the man. It is not the work of General officers to lead bombing sorties but Jimmy Doolittle was not an ordinary General. Twenty times he led out his Mitchells, ranging from Tunisia to Rome, before his next translation. A little before D-Day he was given the mighty Eighth Air Force. This time he was firmly desk-bound in England and, as if to manifest his frustration, he became a hard master to serve. He raised the number of tours demanded of his crews from twenty-five to thirty and ordered the escorts no longer to be sheepdogs to the bombers but to seek out and destroy every German fighter that showed its nose. It was a sound tactic and bomber losses fell dramatically. On Christmas Eve 1944 he sent out the biggest destructive force ever seen, probably the last great air raid of all time. More than 2,000 American bombers guarded by more than 1,000 fighters ranged over the German Reich on which Goering had asserted that no bomb would ever fall.

He left the Army again when the war ended, went back to Shell and became one of the great captains of industry. He is still with us, a man honoured far beyond the boundaries of his own country. The greatest air command of all had been his but it seems likely that posterity will not remember him for this. "Jimmy Doolittle's Raid", small enough by contrast with the thousand-bomber battles, will stick in men's memories long after they have ceased to be able to name the successive commanders of the Eighth Air Force.

He had been as John Buchan made Hannay say, "a decent lad who had good prospects in life before him and had fought because he felt bound to, not because he liked it". The type is not yet extinct.

CHAPTER ELEVEN

The Racing Driver

Edward Vernon Rickenbacker

Among the few benevolent, if unintentional, acts of the late
Kaiser Wilhelm II must be counted his reuniting, for a season,
families separated by the oceans and by the centuries. The
British were his principal beneficiaries as long-lost cousins
from Canada, from Australia, from New Zealand, from various
parts of Asia and Africa and, in surprisingly large numbers,
from the Argentine Republic, flocked home in order to join up.
The wise and magnanimous peace terms forced by Lord
Kitchener upon his own Government as well as upon the
former enemy had made it perfectly acceptable to Afrikaners
whose fathers had served under Smuts and Botha—themselves
now British General officers—to take service in his New
Armies; many respected Boer names appear on the muster
rolls and many of the best of the RFC pilots bore them. It was
not only from South Africa that the expatriate Dutch arrived
before the last battles had been fought. Nearly half a century
before van Riebeeck's ships had anchored in Table Bay others
of his compatriots had been carving out homes for themselves
on the banks of the Hudson River in the New Netherlands.

First among the American names of Dutch origin stood that
of Roosevelt, and first amongst the Roosevelts stood the former
President, Theodore. During his father's lifetime the Kingdom

of Belgium had been called into existence out of that part of the
Austrian Netherlands incorporated into Holland by the Con-
gress of Vienna, and Belgium now crushed under the German
boot. The Seven Provinces were left unmolested being more
useful as neutrals, but with Germany master of Europe it
would only be a matter of time before they went the same way.
When Roosevelt put his thoughts on paper early in 1915 he was
at pains to point out that Old World quarrels were no business
of his and that his blood contained corpuscles from countries
on both sides. The rape of Belgium, however, outraged him
and made for the Kaiser a formidable enemy. In the ex-
President's mind, war was coming to the United States as
surely as Christmas and for the same reason that it had come to
the inoffensive Belgians. "At present our navy is in wretched
shape. Our army is infinitesimal. This large, rich republic is far
less efficient from a military standpoint than Switzerland,
Holland or Denmark . . . at the present time an energetic and
powerful adversary could probably with ease drive us not only
from the Philippines but from Hawaii and take possession of
the Canal and Alaska". In an earlier passage he observes that
"It is amongst those of us who would go to the front—as I and
my four sons would go—who are the really earnest and far-
sighted friends of peace." By 1917 however the old Rough
Rider was in his sixtieth year—just within the limits of age for a
Boer commando—and it became the turn of younger men.
Kermit became the trusty and well-beloved of King George V
in his Machine Gun Corps, and Quentin's untimely death has
already been told. Happily, there was another man of the same
totem at Roosevelt's elbow, ready and able to be the typical
U.S. hero whose exploits every one of his countrymen was
waiting to acclaim.

Edward Vernon Rickenbacker at 27 was rather old for a
pilot. The generally accepted view was that 'under 18 they are
too reckless; over 25 too cautious'. There were, however, factors that outweighed approaching senility. He was of Swiss
descent, the son of a good Ohio family and trained in mechanical engineering which he had studied with the International

Correspondence Schools whose pre-war gift of an aeroplane to the RFC has already been mentioned. In appearance he was sturdy, the kind of man into whose face nobody would kick sand. Early photographs of him in uniform on a Douglas motor-cycle in company with a couple of friends irresistibly stir memories of Victor Mclaglen and Richard Barthlemess, alias Flagg and Quirt.

The petrol engine had no mysteries for him, for as early as 1910 the name of Eddie Rickenbacker was well-known amongst men who wore their caps back to front after the fashion of Mr. Barney Oldfield and raced motor cars. As the 1910 car could move at more than twice the speed of the 1910 aeroplane this was the proper world for a young man of means and mettle to enjoy and in which he could make a name for himself. This Rickenbacker did in a very short time and by his 21st birthday every man who read a newspaper could have told of his successes. He seems to have taken some interest in flying, as did every young man, but it was still in too rudimentary a state for him to be much attracted. With a motor-car attaining the speed of 127 miles per hour in Florida as early as 1906 there was nothing to lure a man away to contraptions that could only pant along at a fraction of the pace. When aircraft could match motor-cars in design and reliability he might perhaps think again.

The early years of the war—the years of the *Lusitania*, the *Sussex* and the telegram from Herr Zimmermann to President Carranza pointing out the advantages to Mexico of an alliance with Germany and possibly Japan in order to regain the territories lost to the USA in 1847—found him in England, calmly engaged in building bigger and better racing cars as the world fell to pieces around him. By April 1917 the fighting aeroplanes of the RFC made those of the brothers Wright as obsolete as the penny-farthing. Rickenbacker, caught up in a war of which he had been a not over-interested spectator, came at once to the conclusion that his part of it should be carried out in the air. There was much brave talk abroad of the vast Air Service soon to be mounted by America—the figure of 20,000 machines was cheerfully bandied about—and a man of his quality and experience must be a pearl of great price.

Rickenbacker returned to New York with the intention of collecting together all his motor-racing cronies and offering them to the country as the basis for the finest air squadron of all time, but President Wilson looked bleakly on the idea. Knowing the passion of French Generals for being chauffeured by the fastest drivers in the game, the champion at once offered his services in the same capacity to General Pershing; he was accepted with alacrity and Private Rickenbacker first saw the back areas of France along the bonnet of the Commander-in-Chief's car. With Pershing as his friend it was not too difficult for a transfer to be arranged and he was duly commissioned into the Air Service.

As might have been expected, he sailed through flying training with the ease of McCudden, a man whom he resembled in many ways. Both understood engines inside out and had a thoroughly professional approach to the business in hand. In July 1918 McCudden wrote of the coming year that, amongst other things, "American aviators will have made a glorious name for themselves and their country."

The heart's desire of General Pershing was to produce in the shortest possible time an American Army, complete in every detail and fit to be at least the equal of all the others. The first formed divisions began to reach France at the time of the last great German offensives and it was an act of considerable selflessness to allow some of his best units of infantry and machine-gunners to be taken away in order to thicken up the Allied line.

Air Squadrons, units in which only a handful of men claimed any experience, had to be formed as best they could be, the one-eyed leading the blind. Only the Liberty engine, whose story is a long and patchy one, was a genuine American contribution to the armoury; Wacos, Jennies and the Marlin machine-gun served well enough for elementary training but the operational units had to make do with such equipment as they could get from the British and French services. But for the

94 pilots transferred from the Lafayette Corps they would have had to be led by men as untried as their last joined recruits. These brought their own jargon with them and in American messes men spoke of "vrilles" and "renversements" rather than spins and turns. It was only sensible that they should begin their service in a quiet sector where they could get some experience at a cost not too heavy until the day came when they would have their own Balls, McCuddens and Guynemers.

Rickenbacker was both lucky and unlucky in his beginning. Because his name was famous, great things were expected of him and the Press had him marked down for special attention. His capacity as a pilot was still unknown and he desperately needed the right kind of coach to initiate him into the business of big-league flying. Whether by luck or adroit management somewhere cannot be known, but his tutor was the best man who could have been found. Raoul Lufbery had been scratching a living over half the world when Rickenbacker's horizon had been bounded by sparking-plugs, tyres and getting from his cars the best performance that money could buy. No two men could have been superficially more different—it is not impossible that somewhere, at some time, Lufbery might have served Rickenbacker his dinner—but they took to each other instantly. "Every one of us idolized Lufbery," wrote his disciple, and Lufbery literally took the younger man under his wing.

94 Squadron began its effective life in a field near Villeneuve, not far from the hallowed ground of Verdun. There Rickenbacker joined them in the early days of March 1918. Their mounts were Nieuport Scouts, the Type 28 which the French had been phasing out since the end of 1916. They were good enough machines apart from a tendency to lose their wings if dived too steeply, but limited in operational value since no guns for them had yet arrived. As there was little enemy air activity at the time—the bulk of the German Air Force was far away making ready for the March Offensive—the first lessons to be learnt touched on anti-aircraft fire and the use of the human eye.

Silly stories were going the rounds about the uselessness of the German batteries. After Rickenbacker had a couple of days to settle down Lufbery took him and another novice pilot out for their first practical lesson. As Rickenbacker settled down into the cockpit while the rotary engine warmed up, the Major strolled over for a last word. "I felt like a man in the chair when the dentist approaches." The orders were the customary ones —to stick close to the leader and keep formation. Once they were near the German lines Lufbery permitted himself to show off a little, looping and diving with an ease that left Rickenbacker open-mouthed. The message was clear: "Don't worry, my son. You are under the protection of a master." Rickenbacker concentrated so much upon following suit that he nearly made himself sick and flew neatly into range of the German gunners at Suippes. Suddenly the little Nieuport began to throw itself about like a dinghy in a gale, with black explosions appearing in all quarters. Rickenbacker, torn between panic and fury with the asses who had belittled 'Archie', was in serious trouble until Lufbery arrived to lead him out to safety. When they landed Lufbery enquired what they had seen in the way of other aircraft. Rickenbacker and his companion, Campbell, both said firmly that there had been none. The Major explained, with his usual chuckle, that during the flight two French formations had passed under them, that four German Albatrosses had shown up a couple of miles ahead and another had been nearer still. Then, walking over to the Nieuport, he asked softly, "How much of that shrapnel did you get, Rick?" Rickenbacker, happily unconscious of any, paled visibly when Lufbery pointed out three holes, one within a foot of his back. The lessons were not wasted.

Not surprisingly, Rickenbacker's attitude to the war differed from that of his contemporaries mentioned in this book. The United States were never in any danger and, except for a brief moment in the Spring of 1918, the possibility of defeat did not have to be taken seriously. Apart from the honest patriotism of decent men everywhere, his main interest was in its competitive aspect. The enemy happened to be Germans; they might as well have been Lapps or Eskimos, so long as they were capable of fielding a team that would stretch his own to the limit. He had no taste for killing; if a pilot were to be shot down, it was a pity, as if a racer had crashed his car through a barrier. Rickenbacker's task, as he saw it, was to be the best flier of them all, better in particular than the best of the enemy. He had the advantages of aptitude and understanding of machinery, his courage was undoubted and he would be joining in the battle at the best possible time. The French Air Service was in a bad way. Guynemer was long dead and the morale of the new men was low. Volunteers for flying no longer came forward and many pilots now were reluctant, pressed against their will from amongst the ground troops. The contemptible performance of the French Air Force in 1940 might have been foreseen had anyone cared to stop and think about it. The Germans too had nearly shot their bolt. When Richtofen fell in April 1918 there were still good men left but the heart had gone out of the service as a whole. American squadrons, untried but unbattered, might before long take over mastery of the air above the battlefields and prospects for 94, with its emblem of the Hat in the Ring—the hat being Uncle Sam's—were bright. At the beginning of April the Vickers guns arrived, the Squadron moved up to Toul and its serious war began.

For the next fortnight Rickenbacker flew regular patrols under the leadership of another experienced hand. Captain James Hall had begun his service in Kitchener's Army as a private in the Royal Fusiliers, probably the only man from Iowa in the First Hundred Thousand. Being discharged at the end of 1915 he joined the Lafayette (where he met his future collaborator Charles Nordhoff) and flew Spads with them for a year during which he was badly wounded. During Rickenbacker's first fortnight, nothing out of the common came to break the monotony and his worst enemies were the cold and fogs that hang around the Meuse. Then, on 29 April, came Rickenbacker's first chance. Hall spotted a solitary Pfalz Scout somewhere over Pont-à-Mousson and moved himself between it and the sun. The pupil obediently followed him. As Hall

began his dive the Pfalz pilot caught a glimpse of Rickenbacker's machine and began furiously to gain height. In the
course of this he appeared to see Hall, did a swift right bank
and put his nose down towards home. This left Rickenbacker
glued to his tail and both aircraft shot downwards at the best
speed they could make. There was nothing much to choose
between them and at 150 yards Rickenbacker tried a tentative
burst of tracer. He was not an outstanding marksman but the
target was easy. As he himself said, it was like spraying with a
garden hose. The Pfalz hit the ground in a cloud of dust and
Rickenbacker congratulated himself on having downed his
first enemy without a shot being fired at him. It was not his
fault that an event so commonplace in other parts of the front
should have excited such adulation. The Press whose activities
achieved greater refinement amongst American forces than
elsewhere, photographed him and wrote him up lavishly,
though never quite up to "Allenby Drives Turks from Jesus
Christ's Home Town." General Gerard of the French VIth
Army wanted to give him a Croix de Guerre but the then US
Army regulations forbade acceptance. It came soon afterwards. It says much for Rickenbacker's modesty and good
sense that he never allowed his head to be turned by such
performances. He knew that he still had a lot to learn.

Early in May their sister Squadron 95 moved in alongside
and another Roosevelt came to smell powder, Theodore's
youngest son Quentin. The old ex-President was keeping his
word. Kermit had left the British service and his guns were
somewhere below with the 1st Division, in which Theodore II
was commanding an infantry battalion. Quentin, like Rickenbacker, was burdened by a famous name but he wore it lightly
and through his own qualities was "easily the most popular
man in his Squadron."

Rickenbacker's second victim, on 7 May, was caught in
much the same way as the first. His section under Captain Hall
were pursuing a solitary two-seater when Rickenbacker, his air
vision much improved, spotted four Pfalz Scouts below them.
As Hall seemed not to notice, his agitated wing-wagging Rick-

enbacker took matters into his own hands and dived, hoping
that the others would follow. The Germans seemed not to have
noticed them, for Rickenbacker again found himself almost by
chance in the killing position above and behind the last
machine. A few long bursts were all that he needed to double
his score. In the dog-fight that followed Hall disappeared. It
was not until a month later that the Squadron learned how his
Nieuport had played its usual trick of tearing off a wing during
a dive. Hall landed in a wood and with nothing worse than a
broken ankle and was taken prisoner. Command of No. 1
Flight passed to Lieutenant Rickenbacker.

He proved a conscientious commander and took great pains
over nursing the younger men. With Hall gone and Lufbery
killed 3 days later it was fortunate that a man of stature was
about the place, for 94 Squadron was beginning to lose confidence in its weapons. Too often did the Nieuport Baby shed its
wings. Indeed men had come to expect it to happen, with the
inevitable consequence that they were reluctant to manoeuvre
more than was absolutely necessary. It was fortunate that the
German pilots then opposed to them were not too formidable.
On one occasion, after he and Douglas Campbell had jointly
put paid to an Albatros, Rickenbacker spoke his mind about
them. "Instead of dashing after us to wreak their well earned
revenge, the four Hun fighters returned hastily to their remaining Albatros and surrounding it began carefully conducting it
northwards still deeper within their own territory. Many times
later did I observe this craven characteristic of the enemy
air-fighters. No matter what their superiority in numbers or
position, if we succeeded in bringing down one of their number
the others almost invariably abandoned the combat and gave
us the field. It may be military efficiency but it always
appeared to me to be pure yellowness." Though understand-
able this was probably less than just, for it was now Germany's
turn to husband all her resources. Even so, it was very good for
American morale. Less good was Rickenbacker's own narrow
escape from death through the usual cause. When the upper
wing of his own Nieuport collapsed far over the German lines it

was only a combination of skilful flying, good luck and great
determination that brought him home. The cry went loudly
up. "When are we going to get our Spads?"

Even without them Rickenbacker continued to add to his
reputation, though the combats in which he scored his next few
victories were not of epic quality. With a better machine he
would certainly have bagged more. It was galling to watch the
Rumpler two-seater blandly taking their photographs from
over 20,000 feet and sneering at him below as he tried to whip a
little more altitude from his unresponsive mount. Early in June
the combination of long exposure to cold at high altitudes and
over-work brought on a fever and he was packed off to Paris for
a few days leave. He did not much enjoy it, for Paris was
crammed with refugees who expected the Germans to arrive at
any moment. Leave, and indeed any sort of recreation, were
things that seldom came the way of US fliers. Rickenbacker
compared their condition unfavourably with that of the RFC,
"past masters in the art of caring for their men . . . to produce a
morale and esprit in the British aviators that has not its equal
in the world." Incidentally, he reckoned General Trenchard
"the greatest authority on war aviation in the world, in my
opinion."

The second half of June was passed in practicing formation
flying, for the appearance of German aircraft in much larger
numbers made it pretty clear that big events were in the offing.
On the 27th all four American Squadrons were moved up to
Chateau Thierry, 94 taking over the French aerodrome at
Touquin, 25 miles south of the town named for the son of
Charlemagne. Though the officers were quartered in a delight-
ful chateau Rickenbacker saw little of it. The fever, never
thrown off, came back and he was whipped smartly into hospital. On 4 July he was allowed to visit Paris again and on the
next day he decided to visit the American Experimental
Aerodrome at Orly in order to find out what had happened to
the promised Spads. He was in luck. Three of them, marked
with the Hat in the Ring, stood on the tarmac awaiting delivery
to the Squadron and on its behalf he promptly took over the

nearest. He was so enchanted by the performance of the little fighter that he did not bother to collect his kit but flew it straight off to Touquin. Like others before him, Rickenbacker had discovered his ideal machine and for the rest of the war he never flew any other. It came just in time, for squaring up to the American Squadrons were German pilots and aircraft of very different quality from any met before. The two staffeln of the late Baron von Richtofen's Circus moved into Coincy, just north of Chateau Thierry, and men like Bruno Loerzer, Ernst Udet and Hermann Goering, in the days when he kept better company, ranked amongst the best in the business anywhere. There was no help to be expected from the French. German and American were going to have to fight it out over the Meuse-Argonne without interference. There was little to choose between the Spad X111 with its 220 h.p. Hispano engine and the Fokker D.V11, though the Fokker manoeuvred better and the Siemens-Shuckert with its 11-cylindered rotary engine outpaced both. Fortunately there were not many of these about. The Germans had all the experience; the Americans were coming in fresh, but many of them were still lumbered with the Nieuport.

On 14 July Quentin Roosevelt, flying the old machine, was shot down in a mighty dog fight by one of the Richtofen men, Sergeant Thom. His father's thesis about America's failure to arm and prepare had been proved most painfully. Rickenbacker learnt of it from a hospital bed; his right ear had developed an abscess and lancing could not be avoided. There he stayed in great pain of body and much more of mind for the last three weeks of July, the month when the tide finally turned and Mangin's tanks burst out of the woods to begin the battles of the final hundred days. The American pilots had learnt a lot during his absence and no longer felt themselves to be minor league players. On 8 August—Ludendorff's "Black Day of the German Army"—the last Spads arrived. Rickenbacker was once more in his old place at the head of No. 1 Flight and only a few intimates knew that his off-duty time was passed with bags of hot salt clamped to his ear to reduce the pain. The Squadron's task for the day was to protect at all costs two French photographic-reconaissance machines. Eight American Spads provided cover and it was no great surprise to Rickenbacker when five Fokkers were seen manoeuvring behind them, backs to the sun and plainly out to get the photographers. Over Vailly the Frenchmen clicked valiantly away as three Fokkers made ready to pounce. With what might have been a determination to smash down the cameraman even though they would go with them or because they lacked respect for American roundels (which Rickenbacker thought more likely), the Fokkers ignored the Spads and headed for their victims. Rickenbacker positioned himself so as to be able to put a path of bullets between the machines. As the first Fokker crossed the line, Rickenbacker's twin Vickers guns gave tongue. Down went the enemy aircraft and all that remained for Rickenbacker to do was to watch a private fight between Reed Chambers and Fokker No. 2, No. 3 had gone off to find friends. Both pilots were of high quality and the battle was worth watching. As the Fokker went down Rickenbacker's engine stalled and he was glad to have height enough to re-start it by diving. Nobody bothered him and the Frenchmen took home 35 pictures of inestimable value. For the next few days Spad and Fokker met regularly but indecisively. On 18 August the pain in Rickenbacker's ear became beyond endurance and he was back in hospital until 3 September. He emerged to re-join 94 at Verdun in time for the St. Mihiel offensive, his ear finally cured.

The 12th September 1918 is an important date in American military history, the first day upon which the US Armies delivered an attack on European soil. Pershing's two pincers, covered by the fire of 3,000 guns, were directed to meet at Vigneulles, thus neatly snipping off the tip of the German nose that poked into France. The first twenty-four hours went exactly as planned and America won a notable victory, opening up the way to driving the occupiers from Lorraine. As heavy rain and low cloud hampered air activity on the grand scale Rickenbacker decided to take Reed Chambers with him and see how far a couple of Spads could be useful. Targets abounded, for the German army was in full retreat towards the safety of Metz, as a French army had been in 1870. The two machines, carrying almost the fire power of an infantry company, raked the road and everything on it for as long as their fuel lasted. Not until the following day did a single German aircraft appear. When they did come they were worthy opponents, four red-nosed Fokkers of the Circus itself. Rickenbacker saw them first—since Lufbery's lessons he did not miss much in the sky about him—and moved into the sun. With this behind him he cut down the first machine without difficulty but then he found himself fighting for his life against three pilots uncommon skill. The old racing driver instincts came to life and it was only the bit of extra speed that his machine could manage that saved him. Even at that moment he was filled with admiration for his enemies as they danced around him, three machines seeming to take up the entire sky.

It was plain that he was still not quite in the top class, but he survived and he studied to improve. Three days later, out on his own once more and in fine weather, he noticed the Fokkers again, six of them this time and more interested in a flight of four American Spads engaged in ground-strafing than they were in him. As the Fokkers went into their dive Rickenbacker joined them, knocking off the nearest with a single burst; the remainder continued travelling East and disappeared. This brought Rickenbacker's total to seven and, if confirmed, would put him in front of the other surviving American fliers. With this went the title Ace of Aces, something by which he set as much store as his racing championship, enough to warrant a trip by road round the balloon stations in order to get the kills confirmed. Lufbery had notched up 18, Bayliss 23 and Putnam 12 but all these were now dead. Luke, in his brief career, passed Rickenbacker but not for long. On 24 September Rickenbacker's C.O. Marr was posted back to the States and the current Ace of Aces succeeded to command 94 Squadron. Pondering on his new responsibilities, he went off early one morning on one of his solitary patrols and once more jumped the end man of a flight of Fokkers escorting a couple of two-seater photographic machines. The other four Fokkers, in accordance with what now seemed custom amongst all but Circus members, made no attempt to go for the lone bandit but set off for home. The two-seater which Rickenbacker then picked was made of sterner stuff. Though he had little enough chance against a Spad, he made Rickenbacker work for his inevitable victory harder than most Fokkers had done. The pilot and observer shared the common lot of their kind and died in the flames. Rickenbacker sent for his car and drove to Verdun where he extracted written confirmation of his kills from a French officer.

The war was now in its last weeks. By the end of September British, Australian and some American troops were breaking the Hindenburg Line and at the other end of the front Pershing's men were opposed only by a few low-grade German divisions. The German Air Force still had its hard core but the apple itself had rotted. Everywhere novice pilots of the RFC were being allowed to attack numbers of enemy aircraft and were having things very much their own way. Rickenbacker adopted a deliberate policy of taking every advantage of this state of affairs. The usual daily forays of the Squadron, protecting bombers (including sometimes those of Trenchard's Independent Air Force raiding deep into Germany) and photographers with some ground-strafing thrown in did not add much to the game-book. When the day's work was over he kept up his voluntary patrols, usually alone but sometimes with a single companion who was more often than not Reed Chambers. These were the times when he could pick his man and add steadily to the tally, pouncing on the unwary and striking them down with seeming ease. At times, when the entire Squadron was airborne, he would hand over leadership to Chambers and move his machine above them as a one man high guard. There he would wait for the dog-fight to begin and plunge down into its heart at the moment of his own choosing. This seldom failed to find a victim and to bring the battle to an end as the remaining Germans hurriedly made off. When the Armistice came his score stood at 26 and his position as Ace of Aces was unchallenged in the American service. The fountain of honour played upon him but, like T. E. Lawrence, he fell amongst writers some of whom blew rather hard.

Rickenbacker's own book *Fighting the Flying Circus* is as modest and as honest as anyone can expect an autobiography to be. The foreword by Lawrence La Tourette Driggs (one looks in vain for Margaret Dumont) is largely in superlatives, including the happy phrase "Never in all his fighting career did Captain Rickenbacker permit an enemy pilot to injure him." The man who had likened waiting for his first patrol to sitting in a dentist's chair would hardly have said that. Anyway, it was over, over there. He could go back, back to the Rickenbacker Automobile Company and eventually to the Presidency of the mighty Eastern Airlines. Further and harder adventure awaited him in the Pacific in years to come but they are not part of this story. He had shown himself an excellent junior partner in the grand combination. Next time the Hat appeared in the Ring its wearer would become head of the firm.

CHAPTER TWELVE

Account Closed

The Battle of Wady Fara

Since the New South Wales Lancers landed at Suakin in 1885 the Australian forces have confronted enemies of all kinds. Fuzzy-Wuzzies and Boers, Turks and Germans, French and Italians, Japanese, Koreans, Chinese and Vietnamese have, on the whole, excited less of hatred than of a large tolerance mingled with a natural contempt for all who have had the misfortune not to be Australian. There have, however, been exceptions.

On 25 April 1915, the day of the landing, a good number of Australian soldiers had dashed into the scrub-covered ravines behind Gaba Tepe and had not been seen or heard of again. No battle between more or less civilized peoples had ever taken place without some prisoners being taken, even wounded prisoners incapable of resistance, and the complete absence of any on this occasion gave rise to rumours that many a good man had come to an untimely end under Turkish bayonets. It was solid fact that the 19th Division had been hurried to Gallipoli in order to thicken up the position opposite Anzac Cove and it was strongly suspected that the 19th Division knew a lot more than it was telling. Many Diggers made a mental note of the number for future reference.

Nemesis was a long time in coming, but come it did.

Throughout the latter part of 1917 and the first months of 1918 No. 67 (Australian) Squadron RFC had been very active indeed as an important part of Sir Edmund Allenby's army engaged in the business of driving the Turks and their German allies out of Palestine. When the Australian Flying Corps was constituted, No. 67 left the RFC and was given the proud title of No. 1 Squadron AFC in its place. The responsibility for keeping the name of Australia in the first flight was considerable, especially so with a large Australian contingent of five Light Horse Brigades watching critically. No. 67 had been an outstanding unit, even in the days when it had been equipped with the leavings of the Western Front and had had no machine capable of taking on the all-German air force opposed to it. So far it had specialized in photography and it had furnished Allenby with the most complete set of pictures produced anywhere of the country over which his army would have to advance. Early in the summer of 1918 the old BE12s were withdrawn and good two-seater Bristol Fighters brought in to replace them. No. 1 Squadron contained a cross-section of all that was best in Australia. There was Mustard, the Melbourne railway employee, Traill, the station hand from Bligh, NSW, Headlam, the Tasmanian law student, Peters, the Adelaide school teacher, and a score of others. Possibly the best of them was Ross Smith, once an Adelaide warehouseman but now a pilot of great experience. Their average age was about 24, all of them being born in the vintage years of 1892–93.

The Bristol Fighter began with a bad reputation, for a two-seated fighter was a novelty and at first pilots used them like any other two-seater, the pilot doing the flying and leaving gunnery to the observer. German fighters shot them down with ease until the Canadian Andrew McKeevor, a veteran at 21, demonstrated that they should be flown in exactly the same way as single-seaters, the observer's gun being used simply as an extra bit of fire power. When he twice knocked down three Germans in a day the Brisfit became respectable. It was the ideal machine for Palestine; it could carry a good bomb-load, it had a long range, and the Rolls-Royce engine was utterly dependable. It is no wonder that this splendid machine survived longer than any other; as late as 1932 it was still flying over the North-West Frontier. No. 1 Squadron was also fortunate enough to get one sample of another aeroplane, quite different from the Brisfit but no less useful. The Independent Air Force was being established at Luxeuil, near Belfort, and furnished with machines designed to bomb deep into the heart of Germany. The Handley-Page 0/400, with four Rolls engines, was smaller than the Gothas that had bombed London and much smaller than the five engined Giant with its crew of nine, but it was still bigger by far than anything yet seen on an Allied aerodrome. Allenby, the most air-minded of Generals for all that he came from the cavalry, wanted some of them and he sent Brigadier-General Borton home to see what he could extract. Borton did not have a lot of luck, for Sir Hugh Trenchard wanted every big bomber he could lay his hands on. He did, however, agree to let one go and Borton flew it back to Cairo. From there he took it as far as No. 1 Squadron at Er Ramle, near Lydda and handed it over to Ross Smith. He was captivated by the great machine and made it his special charge. Smith had come to flying by way of the Light Horse and he groomed the Handley-Page like a charger. The Arab Army felt much the same about it. When, weeks later, Borton and Smith landed the machine at Umm es Surab the cry went up: "Indeed and at last they have sent us THE aeroplane of which these things (the Bristol Fighters) were foals."

For his campaign Allenby had four air squadrons, including No. 1. He had need of all of them, for demands from France had milked him of some of his best Divisions and the replacements for them had not yet come up to the quality of the originals. In mounted troops he was unusually strong, for this was the last horseman's war and the Desert Mounted corps under the Australian General Chauvel – "Light Horse Harry" – was probably the most effective body of riders to take the field since cavalry first made its appearance. It still had its limitations.

One of the traditional tasks for the horse is to get in amongst a fleeing enemy, cut him down and turn his retreat into a rout. This was still Holy Writ in 1918, so much so that the Australian Light Horse had demanded an issue of swords for the purpose. The difficulty, rather obviously, is to keep a strong cavalry out of the battle, fresh, ready and near enough to do its work. Allenby had no doubt of his ability to break the two Turkish Armies ahead of him, the Seventh and Eighth, but to ruin them would be more difficult. The Australians had a particular interest in the Eighth Army as it contained the 19th Division of evil memory.

In the eight weeks before 19 September the RAF and AFC set about sweeping the sky clear of German aircraft. Most of the work fell to the Bristols, which shot down fifteen Germans without loss. It does not seem a large figure by other standards but it represented most of the machines now available to General Liman von Sanders, the old enemy of Gallipoli who had replaced von Falkenhayn in command of the Turco-German forces. To make a change the Australians kept up a steady bombing of camps and communications. The Handley-Page came in very useful for carrying fuel and food on top of its usual tasks and No. 1 Squadron developed an enviable degree of mobility and independence. Smith could not help allowing Borton to fly it but no other hand was permitted to touch the controls. It was his machine; though he still flew a Brisfit with the others when time served.

September 1918 was an excellent month for Australia. In France the Australian Corps had stormed out from in front of Villers-Bretonneux, had taken Peronne and smashed into Mont St. Quentin, the strongest of all German positions. In Palestine, to quote the Official History, "it would hardly be an exaggeration to say that the Bristol Fighters of the Australians kept the sky clear". The Air Forces were brought up to seven squadrons.

Then, on 19 September, Allenby struck. The first blow came from Ross Smith, very early in the morning; his Handley-Page dropped sixteen bombs each containing a hundredweight of

high-explosive on Liman von Sanders' central telephone
exchange at El Affule. Other squadrons of DH9s went for the
other headquarters and exchanges; within a few hours all
enemy communications were paralysed. By noon a small
part of it had been restored and Liman learnt that the British
had broken through his Seventh Army in the coastal sector.
The RAF had bombed the German aerodrome at Jenin and
was keeping up steady patrols in order to make sure that
nothing took off. Next morning Smith and his Handley-Page
returned, dropping two tons more in order to make quite
certain.

The Eight Army was driven out of its positions and harried
by the Royal Air Force as it tried to draw off to the north. The
Seventh Army, to the east of the Eighth, now began to crum-
ble. With Allenby's horsemen cutting the roads to the north it
had only one line of retreat left to it, along a newly-made
motor-road following the line of the Wady Fara and cut out
from the side of the hills. On one side lay an almost unclimb-
able slope, on the other a precipice. During the night of
20–21 September the Turkish Seventh Army and the three
German Regiments making up the Asia Corps set off along it.
The Australian Official History tells of what happened to
them.

"Within less than an hour the destruction of the enemy
began; perhaps nowhere else in the war was the efficacy of the
air force, as a sheer fighting agency against troops on the
ground, so convincingly demonstrated. The main column after
passing from Balata to Khumbet Ferweh turned off along the
Wady Fara towards the Jordan. About nine miles further on
the Wady Fara passes through a gorge and as this was
entered by the head of the force, down swept British and
Australian bombers. Descending to within a few hundred
feet of their helpless quarry, the airmen quickly smashed up
the leading vehicles and choked the gorge. Then, flying up
and down the doomed, chaotic train of motors, guns and
horse transport, through which surged thousands of distracted troops, the pilots and observers continued their

terrible work with both bombs and machine-guns. A disorderly but still united retreat had in a few hours been turned into an utter rout . . . 87 guns, 55 motor-lorries, 916 other vehicles destroyed or abandoned." Then No. 1 Squadron interested itself in the Eighth Army and the 19th Division. "By 24 September the destruction of the Seventh and Eighth Turkish Armies with all their guns, equipment and transport was complete . . . Allenby's victory was almost without parallel in its thoroughness." There were still Australians present who had crept quietly through the night down the deres of Gallipoli whispering shamefacedly that they hoped their dead would not hear them. No. 1 Squadron had surely settled the account.

The effect of the Wady Fara was felt for a long time. It is commoner for lessons to be learnt in defeat, but this time the victors had grasped the significance of it. The Turks had been smashed because they had allowed themselves to be smashed. If they had kept their heads and turned mass small-arms fire on the low-flying bombers they would have had better fortune. It was not lack of courage – nobody ever accused the Turks of that – but a gap in their training. For the next twenty years instructors at Hythe dinned it into their students that the rifle and light automatic are not useless against aircraft; it was always tiresome in the course of a pleasant route march when somebody blew a whistle and all hands were obliged to unsling their rifles, take a regulation 12 degree bead on imaginary aeroplanes, and open rapid, but it was not time wasted. When, in 1940, the dive-bombers came, most of the French army, knowing nothing of the Wady Fara, thrust its fingers into its ears and ran. The BEF did what it had been taught, companies, platoons and even individuals taking their weapons in their hands and shooting back. The Stukas soon became no more than a nuisance.

Ross Smith, the war over, remained wedded to the multi-engined aeroplane. With his brother Keith, also a pilot in the AFC, he made the first flight to Australia in 1919 and both Smiths received well-earned knighthoods. Though Ross was killed in an accident in 1922 before he had the chance to give even further proof of the limitless possibilities of the aeroplane, his name is amongst the very great. But it was not only by their tremendous flight that Ross and some others had shown the world the shape of things to come. It was in the Wady Fara, a dozen miles from Bethlehem.

Bibliography

Archie Macdonnell, at the end of *Napoleon and his Marshals,* wrote the last word on this subject. "I am profoundly suspicious of almost all bibliographies. Nothing is easier than to hire someone to visit the British Museum and make a most impressive list of authorities, which will persuade the non-suspecting that the author is a monument of erudition and laboriousness."

A book as slight as this one hardly calls for a bibliography at all, for its sources lie not in scholarly manuscripts or obscure records but in printed books and in conversations with people who were there, spread over half a century or more.

Allowing for all that, there are a few books that have to be mentioned for their sheer excellence. The Official History, *The War in the Air,* ranks with the Australian Official History as the best and most readable work of its kind. The first volume, by Sir Walter Raleigh, must have pleased his namesake. *Sagittarius Rising,* the account by Cecil Lewis (who, with Lord Balfour of Inchrye, must stand at the head of the RFC pilots still with us) ranks as a classic; Elliot White Springs' *War Birds* is of the same stature. More recently, Sholto Douglas' *Years of Combat* is a treasure-house of useful, first-hand information. Jimmy McCudden's *Five Years In The RFC* can be read aloud and taken in as if it were a tape-recording, even when he says "like a helicopter" twenty years before such a thing existed. His book is a time-capsule, for few men who died at about the age when the law still regarded them as infants have left much paper behind them.

There are plenty more, all of them well known.

Index

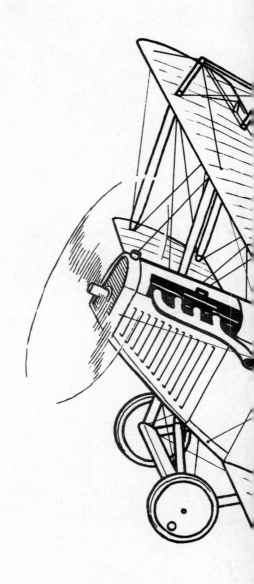

The Celebrated American Curtiss JN–4 "Jenny" (Wing span 43' 7") 1916–1926 was originally a two-seat trainer used by the Americans and Canadians in World War 1. The "Jenny" had a long life after the War as it was particularly popular with the barnstorming pilots of the 1920's.